# Islam's
# Conflict
# with the
# West

# Islam's Conflict with the West

## M. A. Raj

BAKER TRITTIN PRESS
Winona Lake, Indiana

Bible references: NEW KING JAMES VERSION (NKJV)
Copyright © 1982 by Thomas Nelson, Inc.

Koran references: THE HOLY QUR'AN, New Revised Edition
Copyright © 1989 Amana Corp.

*Islam's Conflict with the West*
By M. A. Raj

Printed in the United States of America
Cover Art: Paul S. Trittin

Published by Baker Trittin Press
P.O. Box 277
Winona Lake, Indiana 46590

To order additional copies please call (888) 741-4386
or email info@btconcepts.com
http://www.bakertrittinpress.com

Publishers Cataloging-Publication Data
M. A. Raj
        Islam's Conflict with the West / M. A. Raj - Winona Lake,
        Indiana
        Baker Trittin Press, 2005


                p.        cm.

Library of Congress Control Number: 2005925411
ISBN-10: 0-9752880-9-1
ISBN-13: 978-09752880-9-2
        1. Religion   2. Comparative Religion   3. Islam   4. Christian
        I. Title   II. Islam's Conflict with the West
REL017000

# Publisher's Preface

A revealing indicator of the difference between Christianity and Islam is the intrinsic difference between faith and submission. In I*slam's Conflict with the West* Pastor M. A. Raj presents his readers with the complex roots and consequences of these ancient differences as they are now affecting modern society.

Born and raised in Kuwait of a Christian family, M. A. Raj grew up within the historical backdrop of Islam's conflict with Christianity. He has developed a deep appreciation and understanding of the Old Testament prophets as both their lives and messages are reflected in the lands and societies of the Bible today. Having had the unique opportunity of growing up in those lands, unlike most contemporary interpreters of Bible prophecy, he is enabled to open new windows of understanding for readers of *Islam's Conflict with the West*. With Israel once again a major player in the Middle East after 2000 years in exile we see the ancient cultures around her increasing in their resolve as the West grows even less engaged.

To Israel's neighbors it seems but a few short years since they defeated the mighty armies of the Eastern Roman Empire, forcing Allah's religion of the desert onto the predominantely Christian lands of Turkey, Syria, Palestine, Egypt, and the rest of North Africa. With Europe and its struggling Christian population still reeling after hundreds of years of barbarian invasions, destruction and conquest, the armies of the new prophet, Muhammad, found little resistance as they spread their religion of the sword. Pressing through Spain, they were finally brought to a halt at Tours in southern France. Then after two and a half centuries of stalemate, the Christian West attempted to regain those lands lost to Islam during a short period of ineffective crusades.

Islamic desire to conquer the Christian West had not died. In the 17th century the armies of Allah struck at the gates of Vienna but were once again turned back to rule only the Balkans and Greece. Now, after a few centuries of quiet, violent rumblings declaring the greatness of Allah are once again being heard in Jerusalem, Madrid, London, New York, and even on the Potomac.

As Pastor Raj so eloquently explains, what we are now witnessing is not a new phenomenon thrust upon us by a few thousand straggly radicals, but a true 1375 year old culture war -- and more. It is a war of the ages between the Prince of Darkness and the Light of the World. It must be understood that this is not a media conflict where silent observers will have the luxury of watching global plays as they flip their remotes in boredom and media sound-bite confusion. This is no longer a war of the *remote*. The battlegrounds are in cities and lands where they have never been before. The battle for the hearts and souls of mankind has never been more intense.

*Paul S. Trittin*
Publisher

# Table of Contents

# Islam's Conflict with the West

# Author's Foreword

---

Many are confused when the claim is made that Allah, whom the Muslims worship, is the same God that Jews and Christians worship. Even dictionaries differ on this point which adds to the confusion. Though this book was written at a personal level in my journey of life, it is also an objective look at the history and theology of both faiths.

At this point in world history it is critical to understand the difference between Muslims and Islamists, even though both claim to be followers of the prophet Muhammad. Most Muslims are moderates who desire peace. It seems they hardly believe and consequently do not practice the Koran's teaching about violence. But Islamists believe and practice what they understand the Koran to teach and the life of their Prophet exemplified. They try to obey the injunctions faithfully. Islamists also closely follow the instruction of those Muslim clerics who want to impose Islamic governments that will be based on their personal interpretation of the Koran.

Seldom do moderates come to leadership in the Islamic nations. Today as the West encourages moderates toward leadership in the Islamic world, western leaders are slowly learning to differentiate ordinary Muslims from the Islamists, realizing that the latter have an agenda which takes literally the violent intolerance of the Koran.

In my personal journey of discovery, I have rejected any notions of superficial agreement between the two distinct systems of theology represented by Islam and Christianity because of two life-changing events: the loss of a brother to the Kingdom of Light thru death and the loss of a sister to the Kingdom of Darkness.

My personal journey became painful when I lost my dear sister, Suhba, who came to belief in Jesus, the Light of the World, only to be lured away by the beautiful side of evil. This book is, in part, a response to her questions as she struggles with the teachings of the Koran. I continue to hope that she will claim the power of the blood of Christ to overcome the pride of life and find freedom once again!

I desire to acknowledge the support of friends as this project has progressed. During that disouraging period of losses, Jesus used the encouragement and lives of godly men like Bishop Dale Combs, Bro. C.C., Bob L., and Ryan B. to make my own faith more personal and meaningful.

Sister Nancy B. and my own precious wife, Shyla, also helped make this work a living sacrifice through their prayers, support, and hard work.

The constant encouragement of Dave M., Bill G., and publishers Dr. Baker and Paul Trittin were other important resources in the completion of this project.

During this journey God made eternity more real through the life of my good friend Ron R. This work would have mattered far less but for his life and friendship. Even as he now enjoys unbroken fellowship with the risen Savior in eternity, the memory of his love for his beloved family and his country helped me to focus on the completion of my writing projects. Therefore, this work is dedicated to the memory of Ron.

*M. A. Raj*
July 28, 2005

Publisher's Note:
For the sake of safety for family and friends in the Middle East, all names have been abreviated or modified.

# An Introduction to Islam

## Chapter One

Islam, the submission to Allah, is the fastest growing religion in the world. If the trend continues, statisticians predict that by the year 2050 Islam could be the world's most widely practiced religion.

This belief system is gaining new converts daily including many in the United States, and some have familiar names. Heavyweight boxer Cassius Clay was among the first sports figures to convert in a very public fashion when he changed his name to Mohammed Ali. Black Muslims, a movement among black men, became widespread during the Civil Rights era of the 1960s.

What is the appeal of Islam and its ancient holy book, the Koran? What is the drawing power of its prophet, Muhammad, who appeared in the desert 600 years after Jesus?

What is it about Islam that inspires jihad, holy wars, and attracts new believers in significant numbers while at the same time it is considered synonymous with terrorism by many in the West? Does Islam offer the solution to world problems, as new converts are led to believe, or is it a cause of them?

Sifting the propaganda from the truth is the challenge for today's Christians. To reach those who are attracted to Islam, the first step is to understand the tenets of Islam. There must be an understanding of its history, the hope it holds out to the faithful, and the two faces of Islam, good and evil.

Consider these facts.

**First:** Most people in the West think Islam is predominantly an Arab religion, but it is not. The majority of the billion peoples who follow Islam do not live in the Arab countries of the Middle East. Vast numbers of Islamic adherents live in the countries of Africa and Asia with Indonesia having the largest Muslim population in the world.

**Second:** The Islamic demand for conformity is a major difference between it and Christianity. Muslims not only try to adhere to a strict interpretation of Islam, but they must also conform to its rules and rituals. They are expected to commit to a *practice of rules* instead of making a commitment to a system of beliefs. Whenever and wherever Muslims have been in the majority, there has been a continual effort to create conformity, sometimes by force.

Christians define this as legalism. They believe the message of Jesus freed them from striving for rote obedience to "the law" which no one is able to keep. A commitment to a system of beliefs is a basic premise of Christianity.

The struggle between Islam's two main branches, the Sunni and the Shiite (Shi'ah), is solid evidence that differences still exist within it. These two sects cannot agree on ways to assure *the peaceful practice* of Islam. Violence has often occurred between these two Muslim camps, and it has been that way since the seventh century when the minority Shiites lost the dispute over who would rule the Muslim world. For Muslims there is no separation of church and state; Islam and the state are one. The options are: Islam will use the nation-state to achieve its goals, or the nation-state will use Islam to retain its legitimacy.

**Third:** Of all the differences between Islam and Christianity the one least understood is the use of violence. This is especially true as it relates to conversion or change of religious faith.

In the contemporary media the violent history of Islam has virtually been ignored, but this history is vitally relevant to this century. The media has tried to whitewash recent incidents of Muslim violence as random acts of terrorism by a few extremists often referred to as Islamists. Even after the attacks of 9/11 American news sources have painted a picture of a peaceful Islam being hijacked by these fundamental extremists, the Islamists. It is true that most Muslims are not violent. Most of them do not take Islam as a religion as literally as the Islamists. Nevertheless, Islam *does* advocate violent suppression of its detractors. To deny that fact is to be misled.

In the Koran there is no room for differences of opinion or diversity within Islam, but in reality there is one great exception. The frequent clashes between the Shiites and Sunni, often in the form of civil war, is not unusual even today. We are more aware of the conflict between these two groups when it is occuring in the oil rich countries of the Middle East. Shiites were a majority in both Iran and Iraq but held power only in Iran. In Iraq, the Sunni minority always ruled the Shiite majority until the recent election organized by the United States.

What is the driving force for this seemingly endless conflict?

It is the need of the followers of Islam to create conformity within the total population!

This demand for uniformity has created fear through the use of violence against anyone unwilling to conform to the will of the group in power. Violence has been directed against both Muslim and non-Muslim minorities in most Muslim countries whenever a more fundamentalist group takes power. The Indonesian Chinese minority, mostly Christians, has been targeted. India has suffered a history of violence with Islam although Muslims account for less than fifteen percent of the current Indian population.

This propensity to use violence to cleanse their religion, though not unique to Islam, seems dramatically more widespread in Islam than in other religions today. The West cannot afford to ignore Islam's history of conflict  or its predilection to use violence to gain and maintain power.

How did this conflict begin?

Muhammad, the founding prophet of Islam, lived in Mecca on the Arabian Peninsula, now the modern nation of Saudi Arabia, around 600 A.D. The region was organized culturally along tribal lines, and each tribe had its own deities and idols. The cube-shaped shrine, Kaaba (Ka'bah), in the city of Mecca was the repository for many of these deities.

According to tradition the Prophet Muhammad received his first monotheistic revelation from an angel in 610 when he was about 40 years old. When he started preaching the monotheism of Allah, he was isolated, ridiculed, and attacked in Mecca. After two years of his preaching, tensions between "those who gave themselves fully to Allah according to the Prophet's teaching" and the unbelievers increased. Muhammad believed he had to protect many of his most impoverished followers from the unbelievers. Around 615 he sent them across the Red Sea to Christian Abyssinia (Ethiopia) where the Christian king agreed to protect them. The conflict in Mecca increased sharply as he continued to preach that Allah was the only god worthy of worship.

In the summer of 622 after a decade of increasing persecution, Muhammad and Abu Bakr, an influential citizen of Mecca, escaped to Yathrib (Medina) 200 hundred miles north of Mecca. The Islamic calendar, Hijra, began on the date of this flight, July 16, 622.

Secular historians concur that Medina had become prosperous as a Jewish settlement and outpost for their trading routes. When Muhammad escaped from Mecca, he sought refuge in this city where almost 10,000 members of three "Arabized" Jewish tribes were living. There were also in residence several other Arab tribes who were all jostling for power. The Jewish tribes were willing to provide a safe haven for Muhammad and accept him as an exile or refugee but not as spiritual leader. They were not looking for a new prophet.

When they persistently refused to accept his revelations, Muhammad began to view the Jewish tribes as enemies. What started as religious reform in Mecca now became a religious struggle within Medina. In spite of the fact that the Jews were already well entrenched there when Muhammad arrived, he eventually became the undisputed leader of the city. He achieved this feat through the blatant use of force.

An economic struggle originally existed between Medina and Mecca which soon increased to a crisis level when armed conflict ensued. Eventually Muhammad's forces were defeated by the Meccan army. He blamed the Jewish tribes, his former allies, for his defeat. He claimed their rejection of his message removed the favor of Allah from his battles.

Prior to this defeat in 624 Muhammad's followers faced Jerusalem when they prayed just as the Jews did. According to Islamic scholars the angel of Muhammad's revelation soon instructed him to change the direction for prayer. So in January of that year he instructed his followers to face Mecca whenever they prayed.

In 624 Muhammad began to slowly overcome the Jewish opposition in Medina. The historic split that started in Medina between Muhammad and his Jewish neighbors quickly became acute. There would still be several more years of conflict before Muhammad entered Mecca triumphantly in 630. The once rejected apostate of Mecca would soon become the famous Prophet of Mecca!

Before that happened Muhammad enacted his revenge on the Jewish tribes of Medina. He exiled one tribe, exterminated a significant part of the second, and forced under penalty of death the third to follow him as their prophet. It was during this period that Muhammad established Islam's practice of using coercion and the sword to achieve religious and political, uniformity.

Finally Muhammad made his first pilgrimage to the Kaaba, the *hajj*, just a few months before a sudden illness caused his death on June 8, 632. He had conquered most of populated Arabia for Allah with his radical form of monotheism. The stage had been set. Conflict became the acceptable pattern for future Muslims as they continued in their attempt to unify the remaining tribes of Arabia for Allah. The sword became both the great success and the terrible blight of Islam.

Both Judaism and Christianity stood in opposition to this desire to make the faithful and their communities uniform, but Islam marched on. The name *Islam* is derived from the Arabic word *salam,* peace, but the followers of this new religion would have little of that!

These three great religions of the world trace their origins to Abraham. But there are important differences among them in the ways they understand the experience of God and the fundamentals of their faiths. These differences also affect their interpretations concerning the life of Abraham and the history which followed, causing much strife among all of his descendants.

Islam also gives great honor to Moses and other Hebrew prophets, but it teaches that Muhammad is superior to all those earlier prophets. Jesus Christ has never been recognized as a prophet in Judaism, but he is considered a sinless prophet in Islam. He is even included as one of the six greatest prophets in the Muslim timeline: Adam, Noah, Abraham, Moses, Jesus, and Muhammad. It is the divinity of Jesus leading to his death and resurrection that is the stumbling block for the Muslim.

Each of the three religions places great emphasis on its own holy book. For the Jew it is the Old Testament, for the Christian it is the completed Bible including the New Testament, and for the Muslim it is the Koran. Unlike the others, the Koran is the work of only one individual and consequently it was completed within a very brief period of time.

While both Jews and Christians believe in the divine inspiration of their holy books, neither claims that their text was an actual dictation by God. Muslims, on the other hand, believe God sent an angel to recite to the Prophet Muhammad and teach him. Muhammad, being illiterate, had to memorize the word-for-word messages before he could dictate them to others using his native tongue, Arabic.

Muslims believe the Koran is the last revealed word of God and therefore supersedes the Old Testament of the Jews and the New Testament of the Christians. They believe the words in the 114 *surahs*, chapters, of the Koran are the exact and actual words of God dictated in Arabic, so an accurate translation is impossible because the text would cease to be miraculous. Therefore only those who can read Arabic can properly understand the Muslim holy book. Though it is the primary source of Muslim faith and practice, most Muslims come to understand the Koran's teaching through secondary sources. One considered the most reliable is the *hadith* which is purported to be a trustworthy report of what the Prophet said, did, or approved as *sunna* or tradition.

The cultural bias created by the belief that reading in Arabic is the only proper way to understand the Koran negates Islam's claim to equality among its followers. Only Arabic speaking scholars become authorities. Within this group are individuals from the many different schools who argue among themselves about most points of Islamic faith.

They do agree regarding the salient "five pillars" of their faith.

1. *Shahada,* the first pillar: The declaration of faith by use of a simple formula in Arabic loudly proclaimed through the minarets of the Mosques in Muslim countries five times a day. It is a proclamation about Allah and confirms the unique position of Muhammad as a prophet.

2. *Salat*, the second pillar: The name for the obligatory prayers which are performed five times a day. The five prayers use verses from the Koran in Arabic, the language of the revelation. Worshippers are free to use their own native language for their personal prayers.

3. *Zakat*, the third pillar: The principle of giving alms (about 2.5% of a person's capital). The literal meaning is 'purification' and 'growth.'

4. *Ramadan*, the fourth pillar: The Muslim fast during the month of Ramadan. It is conducted from the first light until sundown each day of that month; feasting is permitted during the night.

5. *Hajj,* the fifth pillar: The annual pilgrimage to Mecca which every Muslim strives to do at least once in their lifetime. It is obligatory only if it is affordable. To be called a Hajjee, a person who has visited Mecca, is a coveted honor.

The philosophical origin of Islam, traced to Abraham by the Prophet Muhammad, reveals the irreconcilable differences between the two narratives in Islam and Christianity. Both of them cannot be right; each religion believes it cannot be wrong.

# Origins of the Conflict

## Chapter Two

Islam's conflict with the West did not start in 1979 when the Iranian revolution brought Ayatollah Khomeini to power. Western media tends to ignore the history of this ancient conflict and consequently misunderstands Islam's conflict with the West. The apparent lack of knowledge of the history of Islam has caused the media to actually reverse the cause of the conflict.

The unflinching support of Israel is not the cause of Islam's hatred of the West. Most reporters and Islamic spokesmen cite that as the reason. The hatred goes much deeper than that. Israel is a façade that covers the true enmity against the West. The Islamic nations earnestly desire to overwhelm the West for it was in Europe that the armies of Islam failed consistently. Their long history of military victories was halted in the West.

Prior to their first major European defeat in 732 at the battle of Tours, France, and later in 1683 at the gates of Vienna, Islam had hoped to conquer the West. Initially the assault on Europe was an Arab assault, but later it was the Turks who carried the torch for Islam. What the Arabs could not accomplish in 732, the Turks did in 1453 when they conquered Constantinople. Soon Arab glory faded from history until the 20th century. Now they cannot even attempt to defeat the West without first crushing Israel, the only liberal democracy in the Middle East. It is delusional to think that the Islamists have given up on their goals of conquering the West.

The fall of Constantinople became a blessing in disguise for the West.

# Islam's Conflict with the West

The fleeing Christian scholars enhanced a Renaissance and later the Reformation throughout Europe. That burst of intellectual and spiritual growth in Europe relegated Islam to a secondary position up to the present.

Islam's conflict with the West has been on-going for centuries. There are five clearly identifiable irritants that foster Islam's hatred toward the West. View them as layers to be considered and laid aside to get to the core of the problem.

*1.* The most obvious is the presence of the nation of Israel in Palestine. The media in the West generally tries to present the current clash in the Middle East and terrorism as the result of this conflict between Israel and the Palestinians. Such a position ignores or discounts both history and theology. The nation-state of Israel is a symptom of the hatred not the cause. Conquering cultures rooted in other faiths is considered proof of the accuracy and finality of their prophet's revelation according to the followers of Islam. The nation-state of Israel is a constant reminder of Islam's failure to infiltrate and subdue Judaism.

*2.* Another contributor to Islam's conflict with the West is the historical inability of its followers to subjugate the West. Islam faces the fact that the West is a civilization more successful than its own and thereby poses a greater question to Islam about the validity of its claims. How could a people that received the perfect revelation fall behind in every sense of achievement . . . in science, in politics, in knowledge, in wealth distribution, and also in military might?

*3.* A third irritant for Islam in its relationship with the West is the Western superiority in technology. It has been this superior technology that has been vital for the survival of the Jewish nation, Israel. Without Western know-how and technology Israel would have been defeated in its many wars with the Arabs. The presence of the state of Israel and the strength of the West are constant reminders of Islam's failures. But the intertwining of those two reminders is like rubbing salt into an open wound.

We move beyond these first three irritants and then dig deeper into the causes of Islam's conflict with the West.

*4.* Creating wealth is another measure of success of the Islamic religion according to devout Muslims. It was initially claimed that Allah gave the oil wealth to the Arab nations to restore the primacy of Islam in the world. That is what they taught in most Islamic schools . . . for a while. But in the last fifty years it is *not the producers* of oil that have enjoyed the benefits of wealth but the consumers of that oil. This created another conundrum for the Muslims. As the West consumes oil produced in the Arab nations, their share of global wealth keeps increasing. The success of the West in creating wealth continues to be another irritant and another failure in the fulfillment of Muhammad's revelation.

It is true that many Arab countries also became dramatically rich, but their masses have remained impoverished. Even the new consumers of oil, countries like China and India with even poorer people, have started creating wealth at an unprecedented rate. For the Muslims, the conflict with the West has become even more perplexing than before.

Muhammad's revelation, the Koran, is emphatic on how the Jews failed God. He taught that God was done with the Jewish people because they failed Him. If God were done with the Jewish people as Islam teaches, they could not have returned to their promised land. If God were done with the descendents of Abraham, Isaac, and Jacob, the Jewish national state would not have appeared in the heart of the Muslim world. So both the return of the Jews to Israel and the resumption of their history pose a deeper question about the type and the veracity of the revelation in the Koran.

Finally the greatest point of contention in Islam's conflict with the West has to do with the nature of God. Our differences center on the nature of God Himself and how He reveals Himself to humankind.

The Arabic language is important in Islam's conflict with the West. It was Muhammad's native tongue and the language used by the angel to deliver the revelation. Its importance is emphasized by the fact that the Koran in any other language is not considered miraculous. In Arabic the word for God is translated Allah, and that is the only name a Muslim uses to identify his god.

The problem is much greater than just the name. Understanding the nature of God is vitally important in comprehending the most significant difference between Islam and Christianity.

The Western notion of Christian monotheism is heretical to the radical monotheism of Allah promoted by Islam. Just as the West was built on the notion of Jesus being the exact representation of the relational God of the Bible, the Koran teaches that Jesus was only a prophet of God but never God Himself.

The god who reveals himself as Allah, in the Koran, is a monotheistic entity that loves only himself. In contrast the West, influenced by Jewish and Christian theology, believes that the God of the Jewish Old Testament and the Christian New Testament is a monotheistic entity who reveals Himself as both relational and caring. The God of the Bible is a God of love – not of self – and full of sacrificial love for humanity.

This deeper level of conflict between Islam and the West remains an anathema for Western media to discuss because it violates their notion of secularism.

*Summary*   Islam's conflict with the West is fueled by the geopolitical presence of Israel, the technical supremacy of the West, the creative ingenuity of the West in creating wealth, and the presence of the nation-state of Israel created and supported by the West. These are all challenges to the revelation given to Muhammad. When power and politics, the trappings of success, are gone, the heart is exposed and the most basic difference is revealed. The true base for the conflict between Islam and the West is about the nature and character of God.

The seeds of conflict were sown when Abraham acted upon Sarah's suggestion and had a child, Ishmael, by Sarah's Egyptian slave, Hagar. The Bible never said Ishmael was not important to God. It does clearly state, however, that the story of redemption will be through the lineage of Abraham, Isaac, and Jacob. Isaac was Abraham's child of promise!

Ishmael, like Jacob, had 12 children (Gen. 25:16), but they were not the chosen ones. Although the descendants of Ishmael are descendants of Abraham, the blessings of Abraham are available only if they follow the God of Abraham, Isaac, and Jacob.

Throughout history the God of Abraham, Isaac, and Jacob prepared man for the revelation of a triune God who through the second person of the Godhead, Jesus Christ, the Messiah, would reconcile humanity to Himself.

In the *relational* revelation of God, the word *love* assumes a deeper meaning because true love is demonstrated in the Godhead. The Father loves the Son and their Spirit just like the Son loves the Father and their Spirit. Their love is *not* self-love. On the cross at Calvary history sees how *genuine* their love and commitment is to each other. This concept of sacrificial love is distant and beyond comprehension in Allah.

The idea of separate yet unified figures in the Godhead eventually became a basis for separation of powers in Western governments. More specifically Jesus clearly taught that the realm of Caesar was separate from the realm of God. Muhammad taught that the realm of the state *is* the realm of Allah, and he used the power of the state to spread the message of Allah.

It was the separation of the church and state that brought the greatest benefits to humanity in the West where people and institutions were granted the power to be critical about faith, thought, reason, and even the centers of power. Jesus taught that power can easily corrupt, so His followers were warned to keep themselves pure especially when power is granted. Secularism could develop in a Christian society while secularism itself was viewed as a corruption of the message of the Koran in an Islamic society.

Like Islam, the early Catholic powers in Europe were uncomfortable with the distributed paradigm of power Christianity taught. But when the monarchical revolutions in Netherlands, Britain, and the United States were completed, most nation-states in Europe copied it. But the states in the Middle East refused to understand or copy this powerful new form of political organization, the nation-state developed by the infidels (unbelievers) in the Western world. At the end of the 20th century, in spite of being granted wealth through oil, Islamic culture and nations were behind other countries in knowledge, ability to project power, social justice, and technology.

The continuing tragedy in politics that affects Islamic nations is the inability to transfer power peacefully to the next *legitimate* ruler unless it is a monarchy or pseudo monarchy. The West is able to peacefully transfer power regularly in their democracies.

Finally it should be noted that the West is not only ahead of Islam without an abundant and precious resource of oil, but it has been generally able to set the agenda in the Middle East's Arab and other Islamic countries. This lack of power over its own destiny poses a unique problem for the Muslim as both their religious understanding and their social setting is weighing them down. The dependence of the rest of the world on oil as a resource for 21st century makes the Arab world vulnerable to powerful emerging forces like Europe and China, both without major oil reserves of their own.

Will the limited oil supply be the dragnet which brings the nations to the valley of Jehoshaphat as the prophet Joel saw? *"Let the nations be wakened, and come up to the Valley of Jehoshaphat; For there I will sit to judge all the surrounding nations"* (Joel 3:12).

# Islam's Conflict with the West

# Final Authority

---

## Chapter Three

Every society has laws, but there is *no society* until at least two people are present. When the second person arrives, conflict is inevitable. Every law is subject to interpretation, and every individual wants to be the final authority on every issue. When differences arise, conflict is usually about who or what is the final authority. It happens between Islam and Christianity, and it occurs within each religion.

In determining the final authority for any issue raised by these two divergent religions each seems to agree on one thing. When a passage in either holy book, the Bible or the Koran, is unclear, accept the practice of the founder or the leader.

If there is lack of clarity in the New Testament, examine the life of Christ. If a passage is unclear in the Koran, look at the practices of Muhammad. The same directive seems to apply to some degree when a section of the Old Testament seems imprecise. The lives of Abraham, Moses, or David are to be reviewed for clarification.

### The Authority of the Koran

If you want to understand Islam, it is essential to separate Islamists from ordinary Muslims. Both groups believe in the Koran, but there are major differences in the interpretation of its meaning. Islamists believe that the answers offered in the Koran are the primary source for society and government policy. It is *the* source for modern life. Islamists replace a rational approach to social problems with rationalizations based on the Koran, the *hadith* (traditional sayings of Muhammad), and Islamic history.

Because Islamists believe the Koran is perfect, they have no reason to have a nation-state making laws in any area where action has already been prescribed by the Koran. Since they also believe all knowledge in Koran is true, it alone should be the source of all learning.

**The Authority of the Bible**

The question of authority in the Bible starts with Moses. He wrote the first five books of the Bible referred to as the Pentateuch or Torah in Hebrew, the foundation of the Bible. The dramatic act of rescuing a slave nation from the strongest kingdom of the day, Egypt, authenticated his experience of God. Similarly his experience of God was mostly lived out in front of an entire nation.

The Old Testament is only the first part of the story of God and humanity. The Apostle Paul, a major author of the New Testament, was not the only writer who was inspired to write about God's continuing relationship with humanity. It is in the Gospels where we find the authentic Christ, the Messiah foreshadowed in the Old Testament.

How did the Koran and the Bible come into existence?

**The Compilation of the Koran**

The entire Koran is didactic, a lecture given by the spiritual entity named Allah. It was delivered by an angel to be memorized by the Prophet. Muhammad then taught his followers to memorize the couplets as he had done. He is its only author.

The believing community is never encouraged to question or critically view the process or the product that came from this revelation. Muhammad was the final authority on the validity of the revelations he received. "This is the way it is because I was told so." There is no check or balance; it is solely the recollections of one man, a very persuasive Prophet. Consider the ego-centered self-aggrandizement of the Prophet receiving this oral delivery which no one could verify. Since the Koran was an oral revelation, how did the written Koran come into existence and how was it compiled?

In the first Muslim *ummah* (community) the key to the Koran was memorization. But some records were kept on bone, camel hide, and leaves. Realizing that many of the people who memorized the Koran as it was recited by Muhammad had died, it became paramount to those remaining that the

Khalifa –
Successor to Muhammad
Community Leader
Title abolished in 1924

fragments of the Koran should be compiled into a single manuscript.

As the hadith records the process, the compilation of the Koran was initiated by Abu Bakr, the first caliph as head of the Muslim world. During his reign (632-634), Zayd Thabit, the scribe used by the Prophet, was asked to search for and collect all of the fragments of Muhammad's revelations which could be verified. According to Zayd, the complete fragments from thin white stones to palm leaf stalks remained with Abu Bakr till his death when they were transferred to Umar and then to his daughter Hafsa.

The second step in compiling the Koran took place during the reign of Uthman, the third caliph (644-656). By that time, the original frail manuscripts were unidentifiable. Uthman then commissioned Zayd and three other scholars to create a single final revision of what had been compiled earlier. Problems arose as five cities claimed to have their own complete compilations of the verses in circulation: Kufa (Iraq), Basra (Iraq), Damascus (Syria), Homs (Syria) and Medina. These conflicting claims were based on an Arabic script which included no vowels. Therefore various interpretations of words and phrases arose which created further seeds of conflict within Islam.

The decision by Uthman to promote the Medina version was opposed by the Shiite Muslims who thought the Kufa collection was superior. Ibn Mas'ud, a companion of the Prophet, compiled the Kufa version and in it gave more importance to the physical descendants of the Prophet. This division played a central role in the murder of the Caliph Uthman. The Prophet's son-in-law, Ali, became the fourth Caliph, and leader for the Shiite faction. The divisions between the Sunni and Shiite continue today, often in the form of military clashes.

To conclude the discussion on the compilation of Koran, the basic claim that there was no discrepancy in the Koran has to be discounted since the other four versions were eventually destroyed. But that is no longer a central point of confusion in Islamic theology because a hadith attributed to the Prophet himself confirms that he had asked the angel to recite the Koran in seven different ways so he might understand it better. Therefore the issue of having only one version of the Koran soon became a moot point though it is a much-touted argument by Islam's apologists.

## The Compilation of the Bible

The Bible is a compilation of 66 books divided into the Old and New Testaments. The 39 books in the Old Testament are sacred Scripture for both the Jews and Christians. The 27 books in the New Testament are written about Jesus and his continuing work on earth.

The Old Testament is a record of the covenant God made with the Jewish nation and communicated to them through the prophets. The New Testament is God's covenant with Christian (gentile and Jewish) believers without geopolitical promises.

The Bible is a unique book, extremely cohesive, and focused on a few major themes. It is replete with historical events much verified by archaeology. It was written over a period of some 1,500 years from around 1400 B.C., the time of Moses, to about 100 A.D. following the death and resurrection of Jesus Christ. The entire Bible was written under the inspiration of the Holy Spirit by more than 40 different authors from all walks of life: shepherds, farmers, tent-makers, physicians, fishermen, priests, philosophers, and kings. These differences in occupation and the span of years it took to write it make it distinctively unique.

The process employed to select and build this compilation of books called the Bible is part of the authentication process of knowing the God of whom it speaks. Unity of the Bible, a persuasive argument in itself, is as important as the canon. Canon, from the Greek word *kanon*, describes a measuring rod. The Bible was canonized. That means it was compiled after it was ascertained by a standard or test of divine inspiration and authority. The rules of this process are found spread throughout the Bible. Although the authors came from different cultures, there was unity in their message. The entire New Testament was canonized before the year 375. The Old Testament was canonized long before the time of Christ.

## The Message of the Koran

There is only one god and his name is Allah is the primary message of the Koran. Muhammad is his prophet, the last prophet of God, and therefore to be believed more than any other. An over-simplification? Perhaps. But easy answers and one-liners always over simplify. It is the superficial presentation that "Allah is great" without revealing his character that rankles Christians and fools the undiscerning. Allah presented in the Koran is not a god of love. He is a god of power and force.

The primary tenet of Islam is conformity to the rules and practices of the Koran. Whatever measures it may take to achieve this is acceptable. Obedience to the rules of Allah is presented in the Koran as more important than knowing Allah. He is not a relational god. There is no invitation to fellowship with him, no opportunity for a personal relationship with Allah.

If conformity is most significant, then it should be no surprise that force is often required to achieve it. We are individuals not clones.

Violence is a doctrinal norm in Islam while it is the exception in Christianity. When Christians use violence, it is an act in defiance of the teachings of Christ and His church. But that same claim cannot be made by either Islamists or even moderate Muslims because of surah 2:216.

Muhammad used killing, stealing, pillaging, and pirating when he attacked the caravans from Mecca with the assistance of his Medinian helpers. He left an example of force that can be followed by the faithful. When he escaped from Mecca, he was persecuted and reviled. But after he reached Medina, he slowly changed his perspective on warfare and included the use of sword and harassment in dealing with his opponents. These aggressive tactics motivated his embattled followers in Medina. Muhammad's only regret was for using this tactic during the sacred month of fasting (surah 2:218).

The surah deals with the special circumstances which forced this early community to fight during the sacred month of Ramadan. Violence is permitted, but the rules of engagement change when it is used against the property of Muslims. A neighbor who belongs to the faith can almost rest assured of great camaraderie; the neighbor who does not believe the Koran will always live in uncertainty. Islamic history is full of events where victorious Muslim communities treat the vanquished humanely. But their history is also full of events when the conquering army is rapacious and brutalizes the defeated in the name of Allah.

The Koran allows these widely varying practices though it has rules under what circumstances they are allowed. When an army practices brutality, historians record it as the effects of war. When a religion permits such brutality, it becomes a deadly sanction for those who want to impose their faith.

**The Message of the Bible**

The Yahweh (Jehovah) of the Bible is exceedingly different. He is a God of love expressed in the extreme by the gift of His son, His only son, for our salvation. God's revelations of Himself and His message were not limited to one individual. He is the God of community. The Biblical version of knowing God is centered on a rational revelation proceeding from God that is given in a relational context.

That relational context was the nation of Israel. This extends from the time of Abraham to Jesus and through the Church until the time Jesus returns in triumph. At that time both Israel and the Church will function together. The great achievements of the prophets in the Bible were not the mere momentary utterance of God's words, though that was of great significance, but it was the presence of God with them. Moses was a mighty redeemer because God was with him when the powers of Egypt were overcome.

The history of Joshua and the Judges demonstrated the same reality which also became very evident in the life of David, the great Jewish king and ancestor of Jesus.

The history of Israel was viewed as the *relational* context for God to teach man about His purpose and plan for humanity. The Old Testament captured it but was not able to reveal God except through the written word. Jesus revealed the face of God, the reality of God working in history for humanity. God became relational in the person of Jesus, dramatically different from any of the earlier prophets in Jewish history or much later in Islamic history. Jesus' message, the Gospel, was centered on the Kingdom of God.

Jesus' life and the message became two sides of the same coin. He literally inaugurated the Kingdom of God into human history. His bodily presence and His relationships with His disciples, which He called His spiritual body, demonstrated that God became flesh and lived among us. The church was born when the same Spirit, that had enabled Jesus Christ to be the supernatural expression of God's relationship with humanity, came on the 120 people gathered in His name in Jerusalem.

The impossible claim of resurrection, hard to rationally accept, yet even harder to deny in the context of history, began a staggering sequence of events. The Gospel He preached flowed out of His miracles, His authority, His terrible crucifixion, and the subsequent experience of His resurrection. Though it was beyond the normal logic employed in the natural realm, He insisted on a new form of rationality open to verification within the realm of faith. Faith was forced to become rational and process oriented.

The Roman Caesar and his Senate, the wielders of the sword during Jesus' lifetime, found that many members of their families joined this dramatic new sect which was supposed to have been crushed by Rome after the crucifixion of its leader. This penetration by a new ideology into Caesar's palace took place without the use of the sword, a dramatically different strategy than the one used by Muhammad. The founder of this sect, the Jewish carpenter, made astounding claims beyond the realm of ordinary logic. His followers were willing to pay the price required of them to sustain the claims of this new kind of power which came from dramatic powerlessness.

At the center of the message of Jesus was the presence of an invisible God who acted in history through His spirit by raising a dead man, crucified by the most powerful authority in human history. This event can be studied through circumstantial evidence as a detective would do. Jesus left behind a radically altered group of disciples who exhibited extraordinary courage in sticking to an improbable story of resurrection. The incredible claim became recognized as truth because of the relationships these disciples offered the communities to whom they ministered in Galilee, Jerusalem, and eventually Rome. Truth was offered in the context of relationships within these new communities. These followers, first called Christians in Antioch, Syria, became the church.

None of these transitions could have happened without the unique role played by Paul, originally an antagonist to the message of Jesus. As a Jewish rabbi and scholar, Paul saw the new sect started by these believers to be distorting the reality of the God of Abraham. But he had a dramatic spiritual encounter with the crucified Christ on his way to Damascus. Then Paul went into Arabia for about three years to meditate on his own mystical encounter in the light of the Jewish Scriptures. When he stepped back into civilization, he came to Jerusalem to present his new revelation (convictions) on what the disciples of Christ were teaching.

**Which Authority?**

Most Muslims portray the Islamists as deviant Muslims who have misunderstood the message of Islam. Analyze this claim carefully, and you will find a major contradiction. A general rule for interpretation is the two-point perspective, the principle of drawing a straight line.

If any text is ambiguous, the second point of interpretation comes from the founder's life and application of the concerned text. All interpretation will be found either in the Koran or deducted from the actions of the founder, Muhammad.

If you want to know if a Muslim can use the sword to enforce his faith and you can't find a surah with the answer, see what Muhammad did to enforce his faith. If the Prophet practiced it, then the faithful Muslim cannot accuse the Islamist of twisting the concerned passage. The Prophet and the *ummah,* his early followers, used the sword many times. Therefore it would be normal for later followers to use the sword.

Christ taught it was important to sacrifice one's life for the sake of truth, but he also made it clear that it is wrong to take someone else's life in order to establish faith. The repudiation of violence was a central tenet of His teaching.

**Rules for Establishing Validity**

The differences between these two religions are not hard to find. The next challenge is to rationally verify which position is more valid. I would like to propose three tests:

## 1. If it is valid, it should obey the law of non-contradiction.

Paul discovered the message of Jesus Christ truly fulfilled what the prophets in the Old Testament had prophesied. Muhammad negated the earlier messages of the prophets and even Jesus Christ by contradicting most of the teachings of Judaism and Jesus.

The most fundamental contradiction was on the concept of original sin. In the Koran, sin has no consequences beyond the person who committed it, "no liability of one soul can be transferred to another (surahs 6:264, 17:15, 35:18, 39:7, and 53:38). Therefore the death of Jesus was not necessary because there is no concept of original sin.

The biggest contradiction in his revelation was the negation of the sacrificial lamb, the role of redemptive suffering as foreseen by Isaiah in chapter 53.

Not only did Muhammad contradict earlier prophets, but he also negated the single most important concept taught by Jesus. The force of truth comes from willful surrender of personal power through a radical dependence on God. The power of truth is negated when trusting the power of the sword. The contradiction in the Koran comes from trying to gain legitimacy from the earlier Biblical revelations while at the same time insisting that these earlier revelations were wrong or falsified.

## 2. If it is valid, it should meet the test of rationality in logic, experience, and history.

The test of rationality of revelations comes by comparing the process through which the two holy books were compiled.

**The New Testament:** As a skeptic, Paul was antagonistic to the Christian claim. But when he reflected on the great expectation of Abraham, Jacob, Moses, Joshua, David, and most of the prophets, he realized that the true messiah of Israel had to solve the problem of self-centeredness in every human heart. Paul compared the life and claims of Jesus, whose disciples claimed that He conquered death, with the promises and the purposes of God in the Old Testament. He concluded that his spiritual encounter on the road to Damascus was real and rationally consistent with the Old Testament.

That was not the only place for this test of rationality on Paul's revelation. In the eyes of the early church Paul was a murderer of believers. Therefore, he was suspect before the apostles and disciples of Christ who led the early church. Yet history notes that not only was his revelation accepted by the disciples, but it became a central part of the New Testament canon.

The process to verify the revelation of Christ included three independent legs, like a three-legged stool, for veracity. The three independent sources that corroborated the collective work of the Spirit of God through the body of Jesus Christ were (1) Paul the antagonist, (2) the disciples of Christ, and (3) the Old Testament scriptures.

**The Koran:** Consider rationally the writings of Muhammad: (1) his experiences were mostly internal to himself, (2) he regularly changed the content based on his immediate need like changing the direction of prayer from Jerusalem to Mecca, and (3) instead of using independent sources to verify the message and the messenger, we find that four different compilations were destroyed to preserve the unity of Koran which in turn was to protect the veracity of the messenger. Muhammad followed a different set of actions. He did not subject himself to any process of verification in the history of Islam as Paul had to in the history of the early church. Finally as the sword in the hands of Islamic warriors brought growth to Islam, it was the coming of the Holy Spirit that gave growth to the message of the church.

### 3. If it is valid, it should solve the universal paradox of human life.

Inasmuch as Islam considers the life and practices of its founder, Muhammad, the authority for resolving any misunderstanding of the Koran, it is appropriate to examine his position on great issues of humanity. Use the same criteria and examine the position of the founder of Christianity, Jesus Christ, on these same issues. Review history to see what impact the lives and teaching of these two men have made on civilization.

Whereas the first test for validity of the tenets of a religion relies on consistency, and the second test relies on logic, this third test relies on experience in dealing with the paradox of life.

The teachings of Jesus were some of the most unusual ideas ever introduced in recorded history. Consider these examples:

POWER: Persuasion and modeling is more powerful than coercion through fear and intimidation.

LOVE: The power of love is greater than the power of the sword.

FREEDOM: The freedom to reject becomes the basis for the freedom to accept.

The study of history will provide the evidence of the impact of each approach.

# Islam's Conflict with the West

Islam's conflict with the West is greatly affected by both the Koran and the Bible. But the lives of the founders have had an even greater impact. This chapter set out some of these differences. The next chapter will consider the differences in the rules and practices of the two religions.

# What is Perfection?

## Chapter Four

One of the great philosophical arguments between Muslims and Christians is the definition of perfection.

**Perfection defined by Islam**

Muslims believe the Koranic text is perfect. However the authenticity of the Koran rests on the words of one man, Muhammad. He said it is a message from Allah supernaturally brought to him by an angel. Access to the Koran is impossible for they assert the original copy is now in the presence of Allah. In true Islam the words of Muhammad cannot be challenged.

According to the Koran the early Arab opponents of Islam and the Prophet charged him with being a sorcerer (surah 43:30,49). The response to this was a warning against those who would reject Allah and challenge the Koran. To those who acted in this manner an "evil one" could become an intimate companion.

This threat adds to the dilemma of perfection posed by Islam. The pronounced curse on the critical thinker adds to the fear of evil, dissuading both textual criticism and independent theological analysis. In the West, the Bible has not only been subject to textual criticism, but it has been subjected to even nonsensical scholarship because of a lack of understanding of rational faith. This intense analysis of the Biblical texts and how it was compiled adds to the idea of perfectible perfection, a concept alien to Islam.

Muslims believe that since the Koran is perfect everything should be measured by what the Koran teaches. This becomes all encompassing for most Islamic scholars as they consider the core of the revelation given in the Koran as the source for *all* streams of knowledge and wisdom. Most attempts to get Muslims to rational analysis or even rational discourse, except to expound their faith, are futile. Meanwhile the rest of the world seems to attain steady progress based on scientific analysis and critical reasoning.

This assumption of perfection may partly explain the rigid adherence to rituals. It is a religion of strict practices, orthopraxy. In Christianity, the Biblical texts point to perfection only in God, especially in the incarnate Christ, which makes it a religion with a disposition towards understanding of doctrine.

## Perfection defined by Christianity

The roots of Christianity are found in Judaism, and so we look at Israel for the beginning of the development of its concept of perfection. The Hebrew *mashiah,* to anoint, captured the Messianic concept over many centuries. Originally, in Biblical usage, it simply meant anointed. It was first used to refer to Aaron and his sons who were anointed with oil to be consecrated to the service of God as priests. Then kings like Saul, David, and Jehu were anointed.

Finally the prophets, who anointed the kings, were chosen to undergo the ceremony of anointing. Elijah, was commanded by God to anoint Elisha, his disciple, as prophet in his own place. The idea of *the Anointed of the Lord* came to be considered sacrosanct: to harm him or even to curse him, was a capital offense as David exemplified in his refusal to kill Saul. At some point in Jewish history, after Abraham and Jacob, the expectation of an idealized king became a central thought especially after the prophet Isaiah.

The scribes called this ideal king, the Messiah, and they attributed to him two natures in Jewish tradition, those of David and Joseph. It was not possible to reconcile the difference between a king like David who ruled in majesty and Joseph who ruled in humility in Egypt as a vice-regent for a greater ruler, pharaoh. If it could be done, it would be perfect. The inability to comprehend the possibility of blending these two different natures into one person, the perfect, guided the people to a surprising conclusion: there is something hidden in this divine plan. It was Isaiah, the prophet, who first recognized that the suffering servant would become the new standard for perfection.

In explaining the incarnation of Christ, the author of the book of Hebrews in the New Testament introduced the concept of *perfectible* perfection, a dramatic departure from all previous notions in religious revelation. Potential for perfection is set in the context of response to the will of God. In Hebrews the theological thought of potential infinity being distinct from actual infinity is uniquely found in the concept of sanctification. This became the new standard for perfection. Even as the Bible taught perfection as the standard, the gap between it and the probable failures in the quest for perfection were accepted as current reality for true spirituality. Thus the journey of faith in life, modeled after Christ and Abraham, was the arena where perfection can be understood and learned.

In most human systems of thinking, perfection is closely related to the concept of the infinite just as we find in the Bible. A similar strand of thought is found in Islam, Judaism, Hinduism and many other faiths. The traditional concept of perfection remained part of the infinite, even for mathematicians till Georg Cantor (1845-1918) introduced the concept of the potentially infinite being different from actual infinity. Until then, Descartes statement in mathematics, 'the infinite is recognizable but not comprehensible' was held true in theology too.

In Christianity perfection was associated with the finite expression (Jesus) of the infinite (God). Jesus fulfilled the requirements for the title of Christ who then became Jesus Christ for His followers. Jesus at his incarnation as a finite man became the ultimate expression of the infinite. As a man, he was put to death on the cross while His character and claims revealed a supernatural strand to His claim to perfection. Jesus became the perfect sacrifice for the Church as taught in Hebrews.

Islam does give honor to Christ, but it denies the fact that he was crucified. They contend it could not have happened because a Prophet of God will not be abandoned to sinners. But they ignore that Jesus overcame death. Islam has no concept of powerlessness as a virtue which is a necessary condition for developing true godliness. In denying powerlessness for God, Islam skews the definition of perfection and Wisdom of God as taught in the New Testament.

**Islam's Experience with it's concept of Perfection**
**1. Spiritual death.** The great tragedy of Islam, the undying commitment to the written word (Koran), leads to spiritual death. The Apostle Paul captured this same tragic mistake when he wrote 'for the letter kills, but the Spirit gives life' (2 Cor.3:6). He warned Christians not to be enamored with the written word above the Living Word. Paul became the servant of a new

covenant, not of the letter but of the spirit, when he discovered the new standard of perfection that Jesus lived and taught.

By attempting to negate the life and teaching of Christ, Islam's definition of perfection was to follow the written rules prescribed in the Koran. This defective definition of perfection in Islam has had five major implications in Islamic civilization. (1) An erroneous paradigm of government was the worst. (2) The Prophet, claiming that he was perfecting what Abraham, Moses, and Jesus had taught, did not awaken humanity to grace. (3) He ruled the tribes of Arabia through revelation to create subjects not disciples. (4) He valued warriors with unquestioning obedience who helped him in battles instead of reasoning subjects as required for a biblical form of government. (5) Truth, rational methods of verification to verify truth claims including standards of perfection were discarded for the sword. Muhammad offered his opponents submission to Islam or the sword.

The Prophet's defective paradigm of power with an excessive reliance on the sword in polity brought initial success in establishing an empire which was one of the largest in history. For them that success became the verification for the truth in the revelation the prophet received.

While the Western world developed a distributed paradigm of power for the government (including separation of powers and the church and the state), Islam continued on the path of kings and empires. It should be noted that even in Western Europe, the nations that gave freedom to the study of the Bible developed the concept of limited monarchy first. It was the influence of the Bible in Scottish history that enabled the church to demand that the king himself be subject to the rule of law. Islam, with a very developed legal system, never was able to mimic or even copy the concept of a distributed paradigm of power.

**2. Unequal use of power in society.** The second tragedy in a poor definition of perfection can be seen in the unequal use of power in society, especially the subjugation of women and the weaker sections of society. By allowing a successful Muslim the right to have up to four wives, Islamic societies were caught in a perpetual cycle of upper class and peasants, a feudal structure for society. Women became possessions of men, not equals before God and the law as in Judeo-Christian tradition. Tragically women have been treated poorly by many societies even where the church was powerful, but it was in the Christian West that women gained most of the modern privileges.

But the greater achievement of the West, the journey to equality for the weaker sections of society, started with Martin Luther's discovery of the key concept of 'the just living by faith.' As in Islam, there was a radical polarization of the faithful after this discovery in Christendom. Catholics and Protestants, from the Council of Trent (1545-63) to the Wars of Religion (1618-48) grew into two camps in Europe. The idea of faith, justification by faith alone, led to Reformation and the monarchical revolutions of Europe. The Protestant nations developed the powerful organization structure called the nation-state, displacing kings and aristocrats. But no such development took place in the Islamic world.

**3. Premature death of science and technology.** The third tragedy was the premature death of science and technology in Islamic cultures. Though they were instrumental in preserving the scientific knowledge in the Middle Ages and in introducing the Hindu-Arab numerals in mathematics in the West, they had no part in the Renaissance, Reformation, or in the subsequent birth of modern science. With the introduction of Arab numerals into Europe around 1000, Europe was slowly getting ready to reap the benefits of the Apostle Paul going to Macedonia with the gospel. Not only did the Islamic civilization play no part in these developments, but they also could not even copy or mimic them in the 20th century. Largely due to the absorbtion of conquered cultures the Arabs became very advanced in mathematics, architecture, paper and even in medicine when Europe was still in the dark ages, but now seem to be lagging behind in both science and industry.

Islam had produced some of the great mathematicians and astronomers of their time when Europe was still in the dark ages following the barbarian invasions and collapse of civilzation. But most of their scientific achievements were based on particulars in certain countries which never became accepted as systemic knowledge as in the West. Many of their achievements, in mathematics, astronomy and even medicine, were real advances in science at that time. But because of the tragic definition of perfection, the lack of perfectible perfection systemic knowledge did not develop as it did in the West.

**4. A lawless society of repression.** The fourth tragedy, almost a paradox as found in Adam Smith's capitalism, was the extreme emphasis on the law. This produced, in practice, a lawless society of repression. After the tribal epoch came to an end in human history or the time of Moses in Jewish history, the rest of the world discovered kings, kingdoms, and empires.

The Prophet Muhammad took the Arabs back to *Sharia,* a legal system based on tribalism. The lack of respect for the humanity of the violator, as seen in the lack of opportunity for restitution, became a vicious form of legal cruelty. The ruling class of priests and princes mostly enforced it on the peasants. This dichotomized society was never able to question their leaders, their faith, or their legal practices. That prevented the rise of a middle class and the restraints imposed by them.

The rise of the middle class in the West literally followed the spread of Biblical literacy in Great Britain, Netherlands and the United States. Thus not only was Sharia a trap of feudalism, it kept the society willing to accept cruelty as part of the rule of law. An attempt to question the Prince or the Mullah priest increased the use of ruthless force to suppress dissent.

**5. Attempt to create uniformity.** The fifth tragedy comes from an immature understanding of perfection in society, the attempt to create uniformity. Believing in their superior revelation, Islamic cultures have fallen in love with a defective understanding of uniformity.

In attempting to create uniformity forcefully they have created a powerful social ethos against diversity. They are also caught in a bloody schism between the Sunni and the Shiite. Though both believe in the finality of the revelation that the Prophet received, yet the Sunni believer does not assign a special role for the Prophet's family in their religion. The Shiite looks to Fatema, the daughter of the Prophet, along with her sons Hasan and Hussain as part of the holy hierarchy. Ali, their father, was killed in the mosque at Kufa, in a religious conflict.

In their quest to create a uniform faith Muslims killed or oppressed their dissenters. Uniformity, the lack of diversity, became a curse and regular massacres were part of Islam. But as the empire grew, it became impossible to create uniformity by eliminating minorities without weakening the state. As an alternative, it was a fairly common Islamic practice to demand conversion. Often the non-Muslim minority faced the choice of massacre or conversion.

Later this lack of respect for non-Muslims took another form. If a Christian saluted the Muslim with *Salam-alai-kam* (Peace to you), the Muslim never returned it. A Christian could not strike a Muslim in a fight without risking his life. But a Muslim can kill a Christian and escape for a stipulated price. Nobody dared to question why the law was unequally applied between a non-Muslim and the Muslim because Islamic uniformity constantly oppressed the minorities.

Real societies are full of diversity even within the Islamic world. This lack of uniformity within the lands of Islam has produced untold bloodshed in Pakistan, Lebanon, and Libya and in the long conflict between Iran and Iraq during Khomeini's time. Minorities survived in majority Muslim societies by paying bribes like the Muslim peasants of those Islamic societies. This situation, though not unique to the Islamic societies, enabled the ruler to use fear and force to control society.

**The contrast in the Western World**

Civilization in the West was developing quite differently as the Bible became available to the masses. Laws were developed to promote economic welfare for the greatest number of people with the least drain on resources. Search for knowledge became a prime goal of society both for the state and in private enterprise. This systematic addition to knowledge about the created world came from a unique definition of perfection. Nature was seen as the other book, created by the author of the Bible, God. Early scientists were trying to understand the mind of God in which the key to perfection was hidden. Unlike the Koran, the Bible taught about the need to understand the mind of God. Early modern scientists studied creation as well as the Bible for that reason. Perfection could be discovered there.

In the book of Hebrews we have the idea of a covenant in the person of Jesus. The author of Hebrews wrote: *though He was a Son, yet He learned obedience by the things which He suffered. And having been perfected, He* X *became the author of eternal salvation to all who obey Him* (Heb. 5:8-9). Though Jesus as part of the Godhead was perfect, He suffered to be perfected as a source of salvation to those who later believed in Him. The concept of perfectible perfection became a model for many of the early leaders in the rise of the West from 1500-1700. Scientists and government leaders became seekers of perfection, both at an individual and systemic level.

Hebrews 7:11 is a clear statement about the law. *Therefore, if perfection were through the Levitical priesthood (for under it the people received the law), what further need was there that another priest should rise according to the order of Melchizedek . . .* The writer went further in rejecting a legal system like Islam or Judaism that cannot perfect the followers with word or code *, for the law made nothing perfect* (Heb. 7:19). Though the author meant the Jewish ceremonial law of the Old Testament, it is equally applicable to Sharia law of Islam.

The concept of perfection in Christianity is both collective and individualistic. The concept of perfection, established in Judaism, came from the law giver and was found in the law. Occasionally the idea of the perfect law broke forth as found in Psalm 19:7, *the law of the LORD is perfect, converting the soul.* But this idea was dramatically different from Koran's idea of perfection studied through words in Arabic.

In Judaism too, when the words became more important than the author, the Jewish authorities did not shrink from suppressing the dissenting voice of Jesus. Unfortunately for Judaism, Jesus made some astounding claims about himself which was to be the new mark of moral perfection. Since the judge of moral perfection was the unseen God of Judaism, Jesus used an effect to prove his claim to exclusiveness. Jesus told his disciples that not only will He conquer death, as the 'suffering servant' of Isaiah and as 'messiah ben Joseph', but He will also start a new age when all those who follow Him will be perfected through faith in Him.

The goal of this age was to perfect a specific number of people, through a new collective consciousness that He was going to inaugurate through the Spirit of God. Later theologians called that process sanctification. Like Moses, Jesus, too, claimed a position of preeminence in the development of a new structure, the church. Jesus used His individual perfection to make an offering to fulfill the demands of the Mosaic Law. *For by one offering He has perfected forever those who are being sanctified* (Heb.10:14).

The process of sanctification is the development of the human spirit within this new collective consciousness called the church. Unfortunately the theology of perfection, seldom taught or understood by the church because of its own checkered history, has resulted in tragic losses for society, especially in understanding the vital role the church played in developing the modern world. In spite of the many failures of the church, many individuals who understand the differences between individualistic and collective perfection as taught in the Bible have gone on to become great leaders in the Western world.

William Wilberforce, Abraham Lincoln, Thomas Moore, Samuel Rutherford, John Witherspoon, James Madison, David Livingstone, Father Damian, William Carey, and many others followed their conscience enlightened by the scriptures in seeking after individual perfection offered by Jesus Christ. Their seeking after individual perfection went against the grain of the collective perfection of the church of their period.

This same phenomenon, a state of being unfaithful, had occurred earlier in Jewish history as the prophet Hosea captures it:

> *"O Ephraim, what shall I do to you? O Judah, what shall I do to you? For your faithfulness is like a morning cloud, And like the early dew it goes away. Therefore I have hewn them by the prophets, I have slain them by the words of My mouth; And your judgments are like light that goes forth. For I desire mercy and not sacrifice, And the knowledge of God more than burnt offerings. "But like men they transgressed the covenant . . ."* (Hos. 6:4-7).

It was the failure of Israel to meet the demand of perfection in the law of God that the prophet Hosea was complaining about. It was never about rituals, it was about the heart.

This failure of Israel became a central argument of Muhammad in rejecting the role of Israel in redemptive history without understanding how Adam had failed in the original covenant. Muhammad developed an alternate set of rituals directing the whole experience of Islam toward orthopraxy. Just as Adam failed with the first covenant, Jesus, the second Adam, met the demand of perfection of the first covenant to inaugurate a new covenant. As the second Adam, Jesus fulfilled the role of the suffering servant to perfect everyone who would choose His steps.

His path excluded religious effort, but it had to be a choice from the heart to follow the way of the cross. Jesus had become the new covenant. The way of the cross produced a new experience of God which only the humble can find within the rich heritage of Isaac and Jacob in Judaism, but not in the heritage of Ishmael.

orthopraxy

**Definition:**
The term orthopraxy comes from the Greek for "correct action / activity" and is used to emphasize the correct conduct, particularly with regards to religious activity. This is contrasted with the idea of orthodoxy, which is about having the correct sort of belief. Judaism and Islam have, historically, placed more emphasis on orthopraxy than on orthodoxy.

# Islam's Conflict with the West

# Two Leaders: Two Leadership Styles

## Chapter Five

The cross is the symbol of the legacy left by Jesus of Nazareth. What is the power represented by that symbol that has won millions of converts to the resurrected Christ after his crucifixion?

Why is the cross and what it represents so divisive and why does it foster such hatred especially among the followers of Muhammad?

We need only to look at the life of Muhammad and compare it with the life of Jesus Christ. The legacy passed down to their followers reveals major differences.

Muhammad was a man who used violence; Jesus was a man of peace.

Muhammad offered a hedonistic way of life: polygamy, subservience of women, force, deception, and power.

Jesus demanded a life of self-denial: fidelity between husband and wife, respect for women, character, openness, and powerlessness.

Two distinctly different messages; two distinctly different challenges!

Submission by force or submission by choice?

Muhammad had established a small but emerging kingdom with a core group of followers and an army that was fanatic in their devotion to him. The book that he produced, which was later compiled into the Koran, was more significant than either the kingdom or the army. The sword, wielded by a fanatic army that gained strength after each battle, would spread the book.

This is in stark contrast with the legacy given to Jesus' followers. They had seen the bloody and marred body of their beloved teacher being taken down from the cross under the watchful eyes of the Roman guards. Jesus, the Jewish carpenter and an itinerant preacher, was rejected by most of the religious scholars because he claimed equality with God.

He had generated great hopes in His followers by demonstrating power over insurmountable obstacles like hunger, sickness, nature, and even death. His followers were pleasantly bewildered by His miraculous power. They certainly expected Him to use it when He was faced with the threat of the cross and the extinction of the movement that He started. In spite of His claim that He came to fulfill certain promises in the Old Testament, no one really believed that included His own death.

There were countless questions. The most obvious, why did His followers stick with their irrational cause in the face of determined opposition in Jerusalem? Even if He had risen from the dead as they declared, what future did they have? He had an ignominious end. He taught for forty months only to be rejected by his own family and friends. His persecutors gambled for his clothes at His crucifixion. The body that was broken on the cross became the central reality for the group of believers left in Jerusalem.

Jesus did not leave a book behind which could be compiled like the Koran. Instead He left the experience of death and resurrection for His disciples' meditation as they read the Old Testament. Paul, a major New Testament author, was not even part of this core group.

The shadow of the cross fell on all their thoughts as they remembered His oral teaching and His life. There was a quality to Jesus' life which could not be squeezed into the Old Testament mold. He brought life, eternal life, and eventually the disciples realized this with a new collective consciousness. Only in retrospection did they understand His intense desire to complete the task of the cross. It was the central aspect of His life for them as well as for those to come. The most intense etching of the experience of the cross into the psyche of His followers was his indelible legacy. His impeccable life before his family, disciples, and followers would have been just a footnote in history but for the experience of the cross and resurrection.

There was no army to spread His message. The followers were not immediately sure what the message was. When they finally grasped that He was the message, the Roman army had sided with the religious authorities of Judaism and together they tried to suppress His stupendous claims.

Eventually most of His followers willingly gave their lives for this supernatural claim: Jesus Christ arose from the dead after His public crucifixion and burial. The miracle of the church comes from this set of events that transformed this apparent defeat into a powerful reinterpretation of the Jewish scriptures and a new experience of God.

God spoke at Sinai through thunder, smoke, and lightning (Ex.19:18-20), but He also spoke in a "still small voice" (1 Kings 19:12). But as this itinerant carpenter, He usually spoke gently, dignifying obscurity and faithfulness. As a teacher, He preferred parables and dark sayings over plain, didactic teaching (Ps.78:1-2). He spoke plainly in riddles but used memorable parables to keep His ideas alive. He contradicted most of the Jewish religious leaders while he affirmed the very Law they were trying to teach.

By not writing books like Moses or Joshua or Samuel, He seemed to emphasize His teaching by the oral traditions. His inner circle was asked not to discuss the amazing experience of transfiguration, a mystical change from the ordinary to the glory of the Son of God, till He was resurrected.

On the cross the gentle voice of Jesus became a gasp liberating humanity from vengeance and the sword. Just as Jesus uttered, *Father forgive them, for they do not know what they do*, the Father's picture, too, changed forever in the hearts of His followers. As the body of Jesus was broken on the cross, His inner-self grappled with a host of the unseen enemies of God even as His feeble voice cried out in triumph, *It is finished!* The cross was the picture of a great victory that Peter took the rest of his earthly life to fully comprehend.

Though Peter and the four evangelists, Matthew, Mark, Luke, and John, placed exclusive emphasis on the cross in the story of Jesus' life and death, the actual event can hardly be understood from their narratives. The cruel and barbaric is written there, but the actual mini-events in the crucifixion we understand from elsewhere. The public humiliation, the stripping of all clothing, the merciless whipping, the nailing of his hands and feet, the long hanging which brought a slow death by asphyxiation because of the failure of the diaphragm are all technical details we learned from history.

Though the evangelists weave the moral and the legal strands in this event, they hardly explained the physical torture involved. The Roman military authorities, the Jewish religious authorities, the established legal system, the disciples, and even the fickle-minded populace all failed Jesus in the last twenty-four hours of his life. As the evangelists later reflect and record in their narrations, they traced human sin as the root cause, but they refused to blame the crucifixion on any particular individual or group. They understood the journey of Jesus to the cross was both voluntary and deliberate. It can be argued from their narratives that Jesus carefully planned His own crucifixion.

It was not merely submission to the authority of God that marked the life of Jesus. It was His *willing obedience* to the purposes of God that was the driving force of His life as the evangelists saw it.

Islam portrays its faith as submission to Allah, but the contrast must be noted. Through Jesus' death on the cross we learn the difference between His joyful obedience to God and the fearful submission to law that Islam demands. Islam treats the glory of God, as in the Judeo-Christian tradition, as being inviolable. But in Christ, both the satisfaction for sin and the self-substitution of God takes the burden of perfection away from man. Jesus, the God-man, paid the price demanded by God's holiness and glory.

When Islam looks at Jesus, only the Prophet is given more importance than He is given. At least for the Sufi Muslims, Jesus is the 'seal of the saints' while for all Muslims the Prophet Muhammad is the 'seal of the prophets' (surah 33:40). All Muslims differ with Christians when it comes to the significance of the cross of Christ and His divinity. Muslims refer to Jesus as the son of Mary by calling him *Isa bin Maryam.* According to the Koran when Jesus, a divinely appointed light, was opposed by the Jews, God stepped into the situation to foil the plans of the Jews (surah 3:54).

So what explanations for the cross are offered in the Koran?

There are four texts in the Koran that deal with the death of Jesus: surahs19:33, 5:119-120, 3:55 and 4:157-159. In the first text we have the allusion to the resurrection of Jesus. The second text states that Jesus said to God "You took me to Yourself." In the third text God thwarts the Jewish plot, and from the last text Muslims argue that God rescued Jesus from the cross. Though there is no uniform explanation to what God did to deliver Jesus, the text makes it plain that according to Islamic teaching Jesus *did not* die on the cross. "But they killed him not, nor did they crucify him. They were under the illusion that they had. Those who differ about this matter are full of doubts . . . on the contrary God raised him to himself. . ." (4:157). It is from this passage most Muslims say that Jesus was saved from the cross because God put a look-alike on the cross.

It is equally possible to interpret from the texts in the Koran that Jesus arose from the dead just as the Bible says, but Muslim scholars never want to even consider that as a possibility. Jesus in this last passage in the Koran is also called the *rasul,* Apostle of God, which is a title also given by the author of the book of Hebrews in the Bible (Heb. 3:1) Islamic scholars are not able to agree on what happened to Jesus' body after the cross because they cannot agree on what God did for Jesus at the cross.

They are unanimous, however, in stating that the people of the Book, both Jews and Christians, will be surprised in heaven because Jesus will tell everyone he was only a prophet like other prophets. If God turned another man into the likeness of Jesus on the cross to fool the people as most Islamic scholars argue, then God was a participant in a scheme of deception. Though ancient Islamic scholars like Ibn Abbas believe that Jesus died for a few hours before God brought him back to life, that explanation is not popular with current Islamic scholars. In the Ahmadiyya movement, founded by Mirza Ghulam Ahmed (1839-1908), Jesus is said to have escaped from the cross to go to Kashmir in India.

What is the true tragedy of Islam in its denial of the cross of Christ?

For that answer we turn to the history of both European and Islamic civilizations to understand how each viewed power, knowledge, and the paradigms of power.

# Islam's Conflict with the West

# Two Ways:
# The Cross
# The Crescent

## Chapter Six

### The Way of the Cross

After Paul went to Europe through Macedonia, European civilization opposed the message of the cross until 312. Members of Caesar's family had become followers of Jesus before Paul was martyred, but the state did not develop a distributed paradigm of power till the Reformation occurred. Emperors could not resist megalomania, and the Roman Senate remained a corrupt body without due process against the emperor.

In 312 Constantine saw a vision of the cross in the sky and the words, "By this conquer." After that vision and although he was a brutal warrior, Constantine made the church an ally of the state and vice versa thereby destroying the message of the cross. While the church forgot about the true meaning of the cross in the West for almost 1200 years, the Bible was also withheld from the peoples in Europe. Through out these centuries the church made Constantinople and Italy the great centers for European civilization.

### Rediscovery of the Cross:

In 1453, after Constantinople was captured by the Turks and renamed Istanbul, Europe was about to rediscover the way of the cross. A twenty-two year old university student was returning to his law school at Erfurt, Germany in late June, 1505, when a fierce thunderstorm struck. Afraid that he would not survive the storm, he prayed to the patron saint of miners, "St. Anne, help me! I will become a monk!" Since he survived the storm, he felt that he should keep his end of the deal even though his family and friends felt betrayed by his embrace of monasticism.

Years later, this monk would discover the centrality of the cross again for Western Christianity by studying the Bible. Against the will of the Catholic Church, he would make the Bible available to the common man. His *theology of the cross* started the Reformation and destroyed the absolute power of the kings and challenged the monopoly of the Catholic Church's power to interpret the scriptures. The monk was Martin Luther!

Christian mysticism is rational though it starts with *let go and let God.* But a rational man finds it difficult to let go. Unlike earlier Catholic mystics, Luther redefined mysticism using logic based on God-given faith and the Word of God. The cross of Christ gave rational boundaries to Luther's mysticism. Catholic mystics mostly focused on the love of God and their love for God which ended in absorption of the finite into the infinite. Because of this, it was hard to differentiate Catholic mystics from the mystics of other great religions. In this environment the attitude of the church made it very difficult for reform to occur.

Luther's most obvious effect was felt in the West. In the next two hundred fifty years it displaced the monarchy-church with a new paradigm of power influenced by the cross.

What Luther achieved in theology in thirty years, from 1520 to 1550, was soon repeated in political science. Rule of law was separated from monarchy. Rational legal systems alone were sufficient to regulate political systems. Power was being transferred to the people, first in the British parliament, then in the Netherlands, and eventually in the United States. Just as Luther insisted that all church teaching was to be measured by Scripture, service to the greater number of people became the goal of political power. The meditation of the cross produced a faith that changed Luther and the West.

The work of Martin Luther insured that the Bible was available in German. Then as the Scriptures became available to the people, reform movements started in France, Switzerland, Holland, England, and Scotland and spread across Europe. John Calvin led the French reformation until he was exiled to Switzerland. John Knox led the reformation movement in Scotland while translators made the Bible available in English.

The English parliament became a bastion of individual rights against the power of an absolute monarch. Each of these movements was led by fallible men who were moved by the cross of Christ. Each movement produced an equivalent political reform movement and a counter effort by the monarchical powers. The modern welfare state, a product of English Labor party ideologues of socialism, got its social agenda from John Wesley's Methodism.

In 1738 upon his return from a missionary trip to the American Colonies, John Wesley heard the reading of Luther's "Preface to the Romans" at a Moravian meeting on Aldersgate Street in London. Like Luther, when Wesley discovered the message of the cross, he became a powerful itinerant preacher whose message eventually changed the face of the young United States. By 1850 Wesley's Methodism had overtaken the larger, influential, American denominations like the Presbyterians, Episcopalians (Anglicans), and the Congregationalists. Methodist circuit preachers played a great role in the Second Great Awakening (1790-1840) which led many preachers to move from the North to the South and in turn ignited the fire of emancipation of slaves. Similarly it was the meditations on the cross by a few men like Jonathan Edwards that produced the first Great Awakening which eventually led to the freedom of United States in 1776.

Why does the understanding of the cross produce powerful mass movements and political reform in the West while no such political reform movements have sprung out of the study of the Koran in the Islamic civilizations?

Islam has no answer.

Similarly the Bible and the cross played a significant role in the birth of modern science in the West as the following list indicates: Rene Descartes, Galilei Galileo, Robert Boyle, Nicolas Copernicus, Johannes Kepler, Isaac Newton, Francis Bacon, Blaise Pascal, Louis Pasteur, Michael Faraday and scores of other early scientists. These men were not only believers, but they were trying to understand the mind of God through studying an orderly universe. When their ideas were scoffed at, they meditated on the cross to withstand the criticism of their opponents. Often it was the definition of truth given by the Bible that kept them from giving up their lonely struggle. They believed the biblical texts even as they struggled against the established church. Just as in early modern science, the order in the mind of God played a significant role in the early philosophers of economics, in the Western legal system, and the paradigm of power enshrined in the constitutions of the nation-states.

The saddest element of Islam is its rejection of the cross and its embrace of the sword. At least five times it denies the Biblical message that Jesus was our substitute, paying the penalty for us on the cross. Islam denies the substitution at the cross by declaring "no soul shall bear another's burden."

Nevertheless the cross of Christ is the pivot of New Testament faith and the symbol that represented the renewal of the Western civilization after the dark ages.

When humanity asks the question why God planned for the cross, the hidden logic of equivalence is at work. A finite mind, the human mind, assumes equivalence with the infinite mind of God. This presupposes that if God were to explain His logic, the finite would be able to comprehend the logic of the infinite mind. This tragedy is most visible in Islam as the mystery of the cross is denied. In Islam there is an ensuing lack of forgiveness in their system of justice. In the denial of the cross an immature view of power became the curse of Islamic civilization's paradigm of power. As the cross uses powerlessness to teach true spirituality, Islam's denial of the cross has cast a tragic web of deception over a great civilization.

Though many lofty moral standards can be seen in Islam, most of it is achieved by the exercise of the highest patience and self-restraint. Surah 41:43 states, "Indeed, if any shows patience, and forgives, that would truly be an affair of great Resolution."

It is more difficult to be patient and forgive than it is to punish the guilty or teach them lessons. But patience and forgiveness would be the best way to get wrongs righted. The Prophet Muhammad attempted this in the first part of his mission in Mecca.

Patience is placed above all the Islamic virtues when you become a student of Islam, and reward beyond measure is promised for it (surah 39:10). But the Prophet himself ran out of patience with his opponents as he took up the sword when he was in Medina. Contrast his success with the sword with the faithful commitment of Jesus to the way of the cross.

Unlike Jesus who went to the cross to illustrate total surrender to God, the Prophet relied on his own resourcefulness and patience. This self-reliance by the Prophet rejected the option of radical surrender to God that the cross modeled. Jesus who taught in absolute terms with moral authority made Christianity an impossible goal to achieve through patience and self-effort. Virtue acquired through human effort, according to what Jesus taught, can be the work of the flesh. The Apostle Paul called the teachings of Jesus *the law of the Spirit of life in Christ Jesus* (Rom.8:2), a product that comes out of accepting the cross into each one's life.

In 711 when Muslims under Tariq entered Spain from Morocco to subjugate that country, the brutality of the battles became part of the church ethos in Spain. Finally in 732, the Franks, led by Charles Martel, defeated the Muslims near Poitiers, France, preventing the further expansion of Islam in southern Europe. In the end it was only the internal dissension of Spanish Islam that allowed the crusading Christian kings to reconquer parts of Spain.

After this gradual reunification, Granada, the last Muslim stronghold, was captured in 1492. Like the conversion of Emperor Constantine, the immediate effect of these wars was the rise of a new form of state religion, a more hardened Roman Catholicism. This resulted in most Jews (1492) and Muslims (1502) being expelled from Spain. Inquisitions followed these hard state policies. An even greater tragedy was the slow transformation of the Catholic Church caused by this continual violence brought into the Spanish church during its conflict with Islam. As inquisitions soon followed these state policies, inhumanity became acceptable even within the church.

Until the message of the cross was rediscovered by the German monk, Martin Luther, Europe primarily used the sword to battle the power of Islam. But Jesus came to fight evil with the Word of God which is the only sword He taught His disciples to use. The evangelist Luke summarized the teaching of the cross in a three-step process: (1) deny self, (2) take up one's own cross daily, and (3) follow Jesus (Luke 9:23).

Jesus taught four truths about the cross; each truth is important for earnest disciples of Christ in working out their sanctification:

1. The condition of discipleship is supreme allegiance to Jesus which includes dying to family, culture, self, and monetary gain (Mt. 10:38).

2. Any attempt to save our life, a characteristic of an intelligent mind, stands in opposition to the teaching of the cross (Mt. 16:24). It is a natural human desire to protect ourselves and plan for our futures, but this is deadly for the discipleship of faith.

3. The cross destroys the love for the world (Lk. 9:23-26). The cross is the set of choices through which we escape what happened to Lot's wife, an attraction to the city of man that she could not overcome. Jesus warned us to *remember Lot's wife* (Lk. 17:32). The reproach for Christ and the rewards for the shame of the cross have eternal value. If we are dominated by our thinking, the love for the world will become deadly because of Satan's scheming.

4. The cross provides a new consciousness of God through a new pattern of life, total commitment. Luke14:26 starts a summary discourse on the cross which leads to this charge, *So likewise, whoever of you does not **forsake all** that he has cannot be My disciple* (Lk. 14:33). By denying this truth about the cross and the impossible conditions imposed on the disciple by Jesus, the church has often reduced the message of the cross to rituals and doctrine.

The cross was God's divine plan to perfect a new order of beings, a redeemed mankind. They are to complete the rule of Christ that He inaugurated while He was on this planet. Jesus called the new order of things, the 'Kingdom of God.'

When Paul understood this element of the plan of God, he wrote about how the wisdom of God and the cross of Christ offend human logic. As Paul wrote, salvation and all the blessings are by faith alone and man should not add anything to the work of God. This truth of salvation, through the work of God alone with nothing added by human effort except obedience, he termed *the offense of the cross* (Gal.5:11b). If we are dominated by our thinking, the love for the world will become deadly because of Satan's scheming.

The enticing side of evil is overcome by the cross alone. The cross was given so individuals could escape self-deception and the sin of self-righteousness, the hardest sin to overcome after the sin of pride. Jesus taught peace with God and with man is gained through the cross alone without fear or guile.

The teaching of Jesus was not dependent on the behavior of the enemy. It was always to be God-centered. Either the Prophet did not understand this truth or as the author of the Koran he had no intention of revealing it.

In surah 8:61-62, the Koran says, "But if the (enemy) inclines towards peace, you do (also) incline towards peace and trust in God. Should they intend to deceive you, God suffices you." Peace is given to the enemy only when the enemy inclines towards peace. The burden of peace is not on the follower of the Prophet. The Prophet acknowledged that deception in peace is acceptable. He used peace to gain military strength so that he could fight better later.

But in his quest for inner peace was the Prophet deceived?

What is the role of deception in Islam?

**The Way of the Crescent**

It is appropriate for the Way of the Crescent to be an examination of the life, legacy, and history of the followers of Muhammad, the founder of Islam. This parallels with our treatise on The Way of the Cross which was an examination of the life, legacy, and history of the followers of Jesus Christ, the founder of Christianity.

Though the approach is similar, there are major differences in the findings. Following Jesus was never coerced; it was always a personal choice. His followers were called to a life of honesty and openness. Muhammad, on the other hand, offered no restriction to thievery or deception, and some of his followers were gained by force and through fear.

Deception, an expression of darkness in human hearts, has many examples in history. Spiritual deception, though harder to detect, is often preceded by an acceptance of deceptive behavior instead of acknowledging it as lawlessness. An inconsistency found in the life of Muhammad was his lawless attitude toward thieving, but he did not see that as moral deception!

In many of his battles from Medina he led his small army to rob the caravans that were going to Mecca. In 624, a year before his defeat at the battle of Uhud, he took a band of three hundred followers to capture a large caravan going to Mecca. A thousand warriors from the largest tribe in Mecca, the Quraysh, were waiting for him near the city of Badr. The long wait favored the smaller band, and the ensuing victory became a propaganda bonanza in tribal politics. It was the battle of Badr which transformed the city of Yathrib into Medina, the city of the Prophet. Medina remained the new seat of power till Mecca accepted Muhammad.

The success at Badr created a division of loyalty within Medina. Many residents kept their loyalty to the Kaaba and its idolatry and left Medina to join the Quraysh in Mecca because they were the keepers of the Kaaba.

Soon after the battle of Badr Muhammad felt his plans to attack a large caravan had been leaked by one of the three large Jewish tribes in Medina, the Banu Qaynuqa, the Banu Nadir, or the Banu Qurayza. The Banu Qaynuqa was the first Jewish tribe to be punished by Islam. After a 15 day blockade in their quarter of the city, they were banished from Medina. In an effort to bring unity to the remaining tribes there a document for governing Medina was created. Islamic scholars came to call this document the constitution of Medina.

Later at the battle of Uhud, the army of Muhammad suffered a crushing defeat by the Meccans. The blame for this defeat was pinned on the Banu Nadir, and they became the second Jewish tribe to be exiled. For two years, until 627, the conflict dragged on till the Quraysh decided to attack Medina again. As the month long siege progressed, Muhammad felt that the Banu Qurayza, the remaining Jewish tribe, was not keen about defending Medina.

After the Meccan army withdrew from their siege, he asked a Sheik of the Aws to decide the fate of the Banu Qurayza. Sa'd ibn Mu'adh has been touted as the person who gave the decision to massacre the 600 men while their women and children were kept as spoils of war and sold into slavery. So the men of Medina's only remaining Jewish tribe were butchered and burried in the marketplace. The seeds of anti-Semitism within Islam had been sown experientially.

Some scholars consider this execution as a common ritual that defeated tribes suffer; other scholars have used this to portray Islam as a violent and backward religion. A few scholars have even called this event genocide, a clear example of an anti-Jewish agenda. While that claim might have an element of hyperbole, Islam has never treated their minorities under their rule with equality. In any case, the propensity to resort to violence remains a key construct in Islamic theology and history, greatly verified by the twenty-seven battles and raids which Muhammad personally led.

**Choosing a Successor: More division**

When the prophet died soon after returning to Mecca, Umar, a member of the inner circle refused to believe that he had died till Abu Bakr shouted above his voice to the gathered people in the mosque. Abu Bakr declared that though the prophet died, the god he worshipped still lives. The Prophet died in the lap of Abu Bakr's daughter, Aisha.

Before Muhammad's death, his son-in-law, Ali (Fatima's husband) and Abu Bakr had many differences. The most significant involved a libelous charge against the chastity of Aisha. Upon Muhammad's death, as a member of the large clan of Quraysh, Abu Bakr was made the leader of the Ummah, the governing council. The fact that his daughter, Aisha, was the favorite wife of the Prophet helped as well.

The weakness of multiple wives for the ruler, Muhammad, was about to show in the history of the Ummah. Abu Bakr's avarice showed itself when he tried to strip Ali and Fatima of some of their inheritance while favoring the wives of Muhammad, since they included his own daughter. Muhammad's family and clan, the Banu Hashim (*ahl al-bayt* or the people of the House of the Prophet) felt rejected till Ali became the caliph after the reigns of Abu Bakr, Umar, and Uthman.

Abu Bakr's two and a half years reign eliminated the 'false prophets' and their armies who rose up across Arabia and beyond after the death of Muhammad. His wars, the Riddah wars, were essentially tribal attempts to keep the loyalties pledged to the Prophet Muhammad intact and to keep the Arabs united in their new found faith.

When Abu Bakr died, the aristocracy of the Quraysh, Abu Bakr's clan, wanted Umar to lead the Ummah. Once again the closest members of Muhammad's family were denied leadership in the religion he founded, breeding more distrust and jealousy.

Under the new caliph, the misogynistic Umar, many hadiths were adopted into Islam which opened the door to the oppression of women. He was an able military leader who defeated the Byzantine army in southern

Syria in 634, and a year later captured Damascus. Christian ethics and monasticism prepared the Byzantines for conquest by the zeal and well honed military might of Arabia. It was his skills as a diplomat that made the non-Arab tribes an integral part of Islam. But after ten years as the head of Islam he was murdered by a Persian slave.

The aristocracy of the Quraysh ensured that Ali was passed over a third time in the selection of the next caliph by employing a process which favored the Umayyad clan. Unlike his two predecessors, Uthman, a merchant, had no military leadership skills. In 644 when he became the third caliph, the tensions within the growing Ummah were about to burst into the open. With the new caliph in place the old ruling house of Umayyad was back in power even though they had been defeated by the Prophet during his establishment of the new faith. Muhammad's clan, the Banu Hashim, was not going to let that happen so easily.

Though the first four caliphs are collectively called the *Rashidun*, the "Rightly Guided Ones", the administrative and military skills of Uthman were relatively weak. He appointed men of lesser caliber, replacing existing emirs in different provinces where Islam had taken root. But his significant achievement, the collection and canonization of the Koran, was hardly a unifying factor as the different regions considered their own versions to be as good as the one in Medina.

By 656 the tensions took a different turn as delegations from Egypt, Basra, and Kufa went to Medina to petition the caliph directly. The caliph became trapped in his home as rebels laid siege to his house in Medina. Though Ali tried to dissuade the rebels from harming the caliph, a small faction asked Uthman to abdicate his position as he was not ruling to their satisfaction. Without offering to abdicate and refusing to fight, he was murdered in his inner chamber by this small group as he read the Koran.

Though Ali was made the fourth caliph in Medina, his granting general amnesty to the murderers of Uthman enraged the Quraysh. Aisha, the wife of the Prophet, rallied these people in Mecca to oppose the new caliph. The multiple wives of the Prophet and their reluctance to grant recognition to the Prophet's only daughter, Fatima, and her husband, Ali, were about to divide the Islamic world into two permanent factions: the Sunni and the Shiite. The people who supported the Prophet's family, Shi'atu Ali (the party for Ali), had a different vision for the Ummah. They did not want to separate the religious authority from the ascending political authority. In history, this group became known as the Shiites, the followers of the fourth caliph. But the three earlier caliphs, the early inner circle of the prophet, saw the caliph's office being different from a purely religious authority. They came to be known as the Sunnis.

But their division became pronounced because of the Kharijites who believed that anyone who disobeyed any of the Koranic injunctions was a *Kafir*, an unbeliever. Unbelievers were to be expelled or eliminated from the Ummah. According to them there are only two groups of people in Islam, either the "People of Heaven" or the "People of Hell." Between their radical view of Islam and the political planning of the Quraysh, it was beyond the ability of Ali to maneuver the caliphate back to religious purity. With the support of Medina, Ali faced the Meccan forces led by Aisha at the Battle of the Camel. After defeating them Ali pardoned the leaders and then moved his capital to Kufa, near the ancient city of Babylon and the present Baghdad.

But the Quraysh were not willing to accept Ali and they raised another army to fight him in 657 in Siffin, Syria. Just as Ali's forces were about to win the battle, Mu'awiyah, the Quraysh commander, asked his army to raise copies of the Koran on their spears. It was generally considered a sign of surrender or arbitration. Though the Kharijites feared treachery, Ali chose to give peace which was based on a Koranic injunction (surah 2:193). But he was deceived as the process of arbitration, after the battle of Siffin, was used to pin Uthman's murder on him.

The angry Kharijites turned their wrath on Ali for agreeing to stop the battle when the Quraysh asked for peace. Later a Kharijite killed Ali for granting peace to his opponents. But the bigger tragedy was the use of deception in peace negotiations even within the ruling circle of Islam. This deception created a division that is still causing blood-shed today.

So why does darkness still rule the hearts of followers of the Prophet even after getting the Koran?

Does darkness in human hearts, inside and outside the world of Islam, have a different reason?

# Conflict in the 10/40 Window

## Chapter Seven

To understand the role of darkness in human history, consider the 10/40 window. It is an imaginary rectangle that extends between 10 and 40 degrees north of the equator, stretching from the Atlantic shore of Africa in the West to the Pacific edge of Asia in the East. At the very heart of this 10/40 window are two nations, Iraq (Babylon) and Iran (Persia), located near where human life probably originated according to the Biblical account. The cradle of civilization, Mesopotamia, gave birth to Abraham the father of Judaism, Christianity, and Islam. The Tower of Babel and the laws of Hamurabi can also be traced to this culturally and agriculturally rich Fertile Crescent. Today two powerful ideologies separate the two nations of Iraq and Iran under the guise of Islam.

It is into this idyllic location the Tempter comes, masking his true intentions. With the sin of Adam and Eve the right to rule the Earth went to the usurper, Satan. The second Adam, Jesus Christ, came and reclaimed from Satan and the invisible entities man's right to rule. Today only a minority of human beings have joined God in the battle against these entities. Biblical prophets kept saying,

> Thus you shall say to them: "The gods that have not made the heavens and the earth shall perish from the earth and from under these heavens." He has made the earth by His power, He has established the world by His wisdom, And has stretched out the heavens at His discretion . . . Everyone is dull-hearted, without

*knowledge; Every metalsmith is put to shame by an image; For*
*his molded image is falsehood, And there is no breath in them*
(Jer. 10:11-12,14).

Yet it is these *gods* who have ruled the consciousness of peoples and nations. An overwhelming majority of the people, ruled in their subconscious by entities other than Jesus, live in this 10/40 window. Even though this region represents only one-third of the Earth's land area, two-thirds of its people reside here. These people live in 62 countries (nation-states), both sovereign and non-sovereign dependencies. If we look at the countries least evangelized with the Gospel of Jesus Christ, 55 of these are among the 62 nations in this 10/40 window. 97% of the 3 billion people living in the 55 least evangelized countries live in the 10/40 window. This closed approach to the gospel is most signified in Islam's great animosity towards Christian missions. North Africa, the Middle East, Pakistan, India, and Indonesia represent the core of Islam. Many people in Islam have seen Jesus as the greatest prophet, even nobler than Muhammed because he is the only sinless prophet in the Koran. Yet they have not seen him as the Son of God.

The Hindu world, with almost 800 million in India and Nepal, in its philosophical aspect is a truth-seeking system but without any objective tools to separate truth from untruth. They worship 330 million gods varying among animals, reptiles, birds, and various forms of human beings. In some form or another every one of these gods hierarchically serves the Archangel called Lucifer, known as Satan. None of these entities tell the truth to their followers because then they would have no followers (Isa. 14:9-11).

The next major block is the more than 160 million people owing their allegiance to Buddha, a person who never taught anything about God. The entire focus of his teaching was right living, but still he had no rational explanation for the evil in the world.

The most unusual observation concerns poverty. Eight out of ten of the poorest of the poor live in this 10/40 window. This gives credit to the claim the poor are lost and the lost are poor, giving credence to the relationship between the gospel and economics. Since Islam, Hinduism, and Buddhism talk about God, why could they not make a difference in the lives of those poor? Christ alone declares His gospel as good news for the poor. Almost 80% of the poorest people live in the least evangelized countries, and 99% of the least evangelized poor live in this geographical area.

God did not abandon this planet or human destiny. From the very beginning of the human story as laid out in the book of Genesis, the Bible gives the promise of the *seed of the woman* crushing the head of the Serpent.

The seed of the woman is none other than Jesus Christ who revealed himself as the son of man and as the son of God who came to destroy Satan, the Serpent. The triumph of the human race over the rebellious angels led by Satan is accomplished only when individuals volunteer to participate with Jesus Christ.

God instituted His intervention program in human history through Jesus while requiring human participation. These people, the people who choose God's will over self-will, advance the cause of the Kingdom of Light. History prior to Jesus Christ was the record of the human experience affected by God through the nation of Israel. The prophets pointed in a cohesive manner to Jesus as the liberator of planet Earth from the evil overlord, Satan. Jesus came to Earth to enable the Kingdom of Light to establish a beach-head. Ever since His return to be with the Father, the Kingdom of Light has waged war against the Kingdom of Darkness. The Bible views human history as a conflict between these two kingdoms (Col. 1:13; 1 John 5:19).

All of this recorded history was enacted in the center of the 10/40 window until 49-52 A.D. At that time the Apostle Paul, who prior to his conversion had been a violent opponent of Christianity, was directed by the Holy Spirit to enter Europe. From then on the most important advancements in political history have come through the work of the Holy Spirit in people who have lived outside of the 10/40 window. Meanwhile Satan continued to hold sway over the people on planet Earth, especially in the 10/40 window.

From 610-612, Satan made his best move by masquerading as an Angel of Light to the Prophet of Arabia. In this guise he either appeared or sent one of his angels on his behalf. He chose a plan through which he could gain the worship that was only to be given to God the Father. His ancient desire to establish his mount above the mountain of the Lord helped him to devise a religious system where both use of force and unequal application of coercive power in man/woman relationships were permitted.

In its purist religious form, this Kingdom of Darkness through selfishness, greed, pleasure, ambition, and the use of force enslaves human beings. In contrast the true Kingdom of Light operates through humility, love, sacrifice, giving, and restraint. The Kingdom of Darkness continues to expand, but that *modus operandi* is going to end at the appointed time. Christ Himself will lead the conquest of the Kingdom of Darkness.

Satan's intention is to hide from human perception and knowledge until the very end, except to the initiated few he controls. The Bible calls these people possessed. As history in the last three hundred years has advanced through nation-states, Satan has sought to dominate history by working through this minority under his control, especially in Islam. Ancient hatreds continue to motivate many of the Islamic religious scholars who control the political leaders in most Islamic states.

Satan, the dark angel, is actually worshiped by the Yazidis, a group of people living in Syria, Turkey, Iraq, and Iran. The origin of many of the Yazidi practices are obscure and defy the simple description of being a fusing of a smattering of faiths including Zororastrianism, Christianity, and Islam. It is a sect the Islamic caliphs of the Ottoman Empire tried to wipe out, and historians say at least 72 massacres were carried out against them in the 18th and 19th centuries. Most of the devout Yazidis in northeastern Iraq have been slain.

The Yazidis are ethnically Kurds, and their name is likely taken from a Persian word for angel. The Peacock Angel, Ta'us, is the central figure among the seven angels they worship. Though Ta'us is said to be the devil, they claim he is worthy of veneration as one of God's creatures who repented and should be appeased to avert his wrath. This is a part of universal deception that insists there is redemption for Satan through Satan. The Yazidis follow a prayer ritual similar to the Muslims, but they miss the most important aspect of evil. You cannot understand the history of the region identified as the 10/40 window without an understanding of the nature of evil.

Other than in geography the dividing line between the Kingdom of Light and the Kingdom of Darkness passes through every heart. It is impossible for human beings to be immune to temptation. Even though most people fail to discern the influence of Satan and the Kingdom of Darkness in human affairs, it is easy to distinguish evil by sin and the failure of people. Evil is blatantly repugnant to human beings except when presented with a beautiful face which leads to the expression *the beautiful side of evil.*

Monarchy was the beautiful face of tyranny. Human government had evolved in Greece to a form of limited democracy during the time of the city-states. But even those city-states excluded both women and slaves from participation, a significant part of the population. This was true until the current form of participatory government was developed in Europe as a result of the rediscovery of the Bible as the Word of God.

As Jacques Barzun wrote in *From Dawn to Decadence* (pg 8-9), the journey to freedom from the rule of Catholicism in Europe started very innocuously:

> "Henry VIII, sincerely convinced that his marriage to Queen
> Catherine was incestuous and prevented his begetting a male heir,
> asked the pope for an annulment at a time when Lutheran ideas

were spreading. The king had previously attacked Luther in a learned tract, for which the pope had named Henry 'Defender of the Faith.' Now the defender had to break with a pope who dared not grant the divorce because Emperor Charles V would not hear of it: Catherine was his aunt. Out of this operatic plot came a new church, the Anglican Church, headed by the king, not a cleric, and forever independent of Rome."

The Reformation in England, a seesaw battle from 1531 to 1580, was consolidated under Queen Elizabeth I. The Anglican Church, the state sponsored Church of England, became politically powerful. It is primarily Calvinistic in doctrine but Episcopal in government and liturgy like the Catholic Church. The Anglican Church played an important role in limiting the power of monarchy and the powerful Catholic Church in Europe. Soon after Luther left the scene, the Protestant Reformation made great strides in the first generation even though the Roman Catholic Church tried to squelch it.

Catholicism, a centralizing force, unleashed all its power to destroy Protestantism, crush the many Protestant churches, and conquer the lost territories of the mother church. The great conflict spanned more than a century, 1521-1648. The second half of this struggle became a great war of extermination of Protestants ending in 1648 with the Peace of Westphalia. This last period from 1618 to 1648, is called the Thirty Years' War. Though neither side won, Protestant nations were established throughout the edges of Western and Northern Europe. The Scandinavian countries, two-thirds of Germany, most of Switzerland, all of Holland, and all of England and Scotland, and sections in France and Hungary, became Protestant while the first nation-state in North America was being populated by Protestants. The rest of Europe, mostly the old Europe of France, Spain, Portugal, Italy, Austria, Bohemia, and Poland, remained strongly Catholic.

The Reformation powered the political progress in Europe as the Bible was made available to the common man. Gradually these freedoms led to the textual criticism of the Bible, especially in Germany. Unfortunately this unbridled trend led to the rise of the occult and finally Nazism in the first half of 20th century.

These developments in Europe, spread over the past 500 years, stemming from the rediscovery of the Bible, created the current global culture of the 21st century and freed the Western governments from Catholicism and monarchical tyranny. But from God's perspective, the people in the 10/40 window, especially the Middle East, are still under the grip of superstitions originating from various pagan religions. In the Middle East and many parts of Asia, Islam uses biblical characters and terminology to keep its paganism hidden. The first half of the 21$^{st}$ century may seem to be the time when the Asian countries will be liberated from the power of Islam, the last of the great giants that opposes the knowledge of the God of the Bible. Unlike Catholicism which never opposed the spread of the Name of God, only the Word of God, Islam opposes both the Word of God and the Name of God.

Just as northern Europe was freed from the clutches of superstition through a long conflict, the Bible predicts a terrible season of war when the minds of the people of the Middle East are going to be freed from their bondage to false gods. The Old Testament prophets saw how the Jewish nation, Israel, will play a central role in these events. Also the growing need for oil, as global consumption increases, might be an economic reason for this spiritual conflict. The Bible predicts a great future for humanity when sin and superstition are banished with the Righteous King ruling the Earth from Jerusalem.

The ancient enemy of man and God, as Martin Luther discovered in the early 1500s, has not left the scene. He carefully works behind the scenes as he did in Luther's Germany before the rise of Nazism in the 20$^{th}$ century. The huge volume of textual criticism of the Bible in 19$^{th}$ century Germany discredited the Bible making the nihilistic works of philosophers the basis of intellectual life in the early 20$^{th}$ century. Martin Luther was a forgotten hero as occult and Eastern spirituality spread through Germany just before the rise of Nazism. As the Bible was forgotten, Adolf Hitler used the symbol of the broken cross, obtaining church support in his fight against Communism in the streets of Germany. As Hitler's plans unfolded, he kept his hatred of the Jew hidden from most of his admirers. The dark consciousness that controlled Hitler in the end was far more focused on destroying European Jewry than granting him the leadership of Europe and the world.

This consciousness that enveloped Hitler still works through the beautiful side of Islam in the Middle East. What is hidden by Islam is its torrent of hatred of the Jew and the Jewish state, Israel. Thus most reformers within Islam who preach tolerance toward the Jews get assassinated or silenced by the Islamists. The moderates within Islam who view politics and religion as two separate realms do not have the ability to reform the core of Islam. The politicians within Islamic societies, who are willing to take a critical look at Islamic theology and the Jewish nation, will not get re-elected to create an atmosphere for change. It almost seems that the hidden consciousness that works as the power of lawlessness can hijack the ideology of Islam to create world conditions similar to those which led to the rise of Hitler.

The largest human systems that exist today are the nation-states. The behavior of each nation-state can be correlated to the understanding of evil shared by its majority. The prevailing understanding of evil comes from the religious faith of the majority or an influential minority holding power. As a system of faith, Islam controls more nation-states than any other philosophy today. Yet the most powerful nation-states exist in the West where unfortunately the Christian concept of evil has almost vanished from the modern worldview. Ironically the only two exceptions in the West seem to be the United States and the nations that still owe allegiance to Catholicism.

The totalitarian nation-states are blatant about their disregard for truth. But a few nation-states like the Great Britain, Netherlands, France, Germany, Japan, Israel, and the United States now have a higher regard for the rule of law and its practice. Yet both Japan and Israel have a comparatively shorter history with the rule of law while Germany suffered a complete break down in its rule of law under the Nazis. When rule of law breaks down, the first casualty is truth.

In the Islamic world, even where there is a stable form of government, there is an utter lack of self-criticism. This lack always provides the ideology for tyranny. Conversely the presence of rule of law does not prevent Satan from working within a free society. A very successful model used by Satan to break apart a law-abiding nation-state is through the rise to power of a highly organized minority. This concept, coup d'état, was used by Hitler in Germany. His revolution was unleashed after capturing power through election and politics.

Unlike Hitler's use of the political system, most revolutionaries in the Islamic world, in the 20th century succeeded overthrowing constitutions by force. Like Hitler many have tried to export their revolution as Khomeini, Saddam, and Nasser did. In the Islamic world only revolutions with a religious ideology have demonstrated the will to create lasting tyranny. The apathy towards life and the rule of law in Islamic states is often the consequence of rejection of truth in the religious arena.

The journey to political freedom, the displacement of a monarchical form of government, started in Europe after Luther challenged Catholicism. Is it possible a similar journey has started in the Islamic world with the overthrow of Saddam Hussein?

Just as Catholicism kept Europe under a dark cloud for almost a thousand years, till 1500, Islam has kept the Middle East under its wrap for more than a thousand years. Though this ancient conflict, which the Bible calls a mystery, is not easy to understand, it is fairly well laid out in many steps and stages that will unfold as this spiritual conflict gets resolved. The Mystery of Lawlessness that Paul referred to in 2 Thessalonians 2:7 is going to be solved when the unseen host of wickedness that prompts the nations to act against the true God are finally defeated.

The Prophet Isaiah is specific about the different major cities and states around Israel to be in the final action God initiates against these entities that rule the Middle East. He wrote that a future civil war in Egypt is inevitable as God comes to judge that civilization: . . .

> Behold, the LORD rides on a swift cloud, And will come into Egypt; The idols of Egypt will totter at His presence, And the heart of Egypt will melt in its midst. "I will set Egyptians against Egyptians; Everyone will fight against his brother, And everyone against his neighbor, City against city, kingdom against kingdom. The spirit of Egypt will fail in its midst; I will destroy their counsel, And they will consult the idols and the charmers, The mediums and the sorcerers. And the Egyptians I will give Into the hand of a cruel master, And a fierce king will rule over them," Says the Lord, the LORD of hosts . . . Where are they? Where are your wise men? Let them tell you now, And let them know what the LORD of hosts has purposed against Egypt (Isa. 19:1-4, 12).

Even as the nation-states are struggling with the on-going war in Iraq, the Bible is emphatic that a future king, a tyrant, will rule Egypt in the context of a civil war. The identity of this tyrant, though not well laid out, almost certainly overlaps with the same king who will oppress the nation Israel in the Prophet Daniel's 70-week prophecy. Daniel calls this terrible ruler "*the prince who is to come*" (Dan.9:26). As this future tyrant offers peace in the Middle East, both Israel and Egypt will be fooled by his terms of peace as the Temple Mount is offered to the Jew to build his long awaited Third Temple. Isaiah clearly states the amazing process of deliverance will start in Egypt for the people who call on Allah, who is probably the ancient moon god, who previously worked through Ba'al and Bel.

> In that day there will be an altar to the LORD in the midst of the land of Egypt, and a pillar to the LORD at its border. And it will be for a sign and for a witness to the LORD of hosts in the land of Egypt; for they will cry to the LORD because of the oppressors, and He will send them a Savior and a Mighty One, and He will deliver them. Then the LORD will be known to Egypt, and the Egyptians will know the LORD in that day, and will make sacrifice and offering; yes, they will make a vow to the LORD and

*perform it. And the LORD will strike Egypt, He will strike and heal it; they will return to the LORD, and He will be entreated by them and heal them. In that day there will be a highway from Egypt to Assyria, and the Assyrian will come into Egypt and the Egyptian into Assyria, and the Egyptians will serve with the Assyrians. In that day Israel will be one of three with Egypt and Assyria—a blessing in the midst of the land, whom the LORD of hosts shall bless, saying, "Blessed is Egypt My people, and Assyria the work of My hands, and Israel My inheritance"* (Isa. 19:19-25).

Isaiah saw the eventual triumph of the truth of the God of Abraham, Isaac, and Jacob because the Egyptians will cry out for deliverance from their oppressors which includes their current gods and a European tyrant yet to appear on the scene. Satan, the ancient foe of God and man, will keep trying to prove that he is still god-like while his doom will include the fate of an ordinary man. *"Will you still say before him who slays you, 'I am a god'? But you shall be a man, and not a god, In the hand of him who slays you"* (Ezek. 28:9).

Will the Christian world awaken to what is happening in the 10/40 window?

# Islam's Conflict with the West

# Which Angel?

---

## Chapter Eight

Are all angels sent by God?

How do we know where angels are from?

Is an abnormal physical reaction proof of an angelic visitation?

Under what circumstances do you accept the unverifiable testimony of one individual?

Under what conditions should the advice of an unidentifiable angel be followed?

Unanswered but not unanswerable!

Of the three classic examples of deception in the Bible the first two are in the book of Genesis. In the first instance when the human fall began, the enemy of humanity used both deception and half-truths to get Eve to doubt God. He did not identify himself as a rebel, and he did not shed his masquerade as the serpent. By creating intellectual doubt, he was able to manipulate her will to act in rebellion against God. If the adversary manipulated Eve, the true rebel was Adam. He deliberated before choosing Eve over God thereby giving credence to his own ego-centricity. Rebellion in Adam's family increased to eventually include murder when his son, Cain, killed his brother, Abel.

The second instance of deception was when Isaac's younger son, Jacob, deceived his elderly father to gain the blessings intended for his older sibling, Esau. In this instance the perpetrator becomes a fugitive, a type for all of humanity that is trying to escape from the presence of God. Though Islam shares many concepts with Christianity, it does not share the concept of original sin or the gravity of self-deception.

The third instance of deception in the Bible occurred within the inner circle of the first twelve disciples. Judas' deceptive greeting, "Friend," had the most lasting impact. Moved by greed the blood-tinged thirty pieces of silver are symbolic of the bargain price all humanity willingly accepts to silence their conscience in order to enjoy the temporal security of material blessings. Truth doesn't even try to get a second chance.

Deception is a central theme of the human drama in the Bible. In Islam it is even seen in the peace-making tradition. What does the Koran have to say about deception?

The preeminent concept in Islam, the doctrine of one God, *Tawhid* (also called *al Kalaam*), is their hatred for idols and idolatry. As a religion, it opposes all forms of idolatry while it insists that the fifth pillar of Islam in the rites of Hajj cannot be completed without circling the Kaaba seven times, sometimes kissing the ancient black stone which is embedded in its outer wall as prescribed by Muhammad, or going seven times between the mountains of Safa and Marwa like Hagar, the mother of Ishmael. Worship of objects seems to happen in Islam without really calling it idolatry.

Whatever may be the philosophical and theological arguments of Islam, the entire faith seems to be self-deceived in their hatred of idolatry while they unwittingly keep going around a structure with its pre-Islamic black stone in the worship of their god. Is this god, the God of Abraham as claimed by the angel who taught the Prophet Muhammad? In exploring this contradiction along with the other differences between the two narratives of Islam and Christianity, we find the theory of evil described in the Bible significantly proven by Islam. We start our analysis with the introduction to the surahs in the Koran (C 29-31).

> The Chosen One was in the Cave of Hira. For two years and more he had prayed, adored his Creator, and wondered at the mystery of man with his corruptible flesh, just growing out of a clot, and the soul in him reaching out to knowledge sublime, new and ever new, taught by the bounty of Allah, and leading to that which man himself knoweth not. And now, behold! a dazzling vision of beauty and light overpowered his senses, and he heard the word '*Iqra!*' when interpreted may mean read, proclaim, or recite.
>
> The unlettered Prophet was puzzled; he could not read. The angel seemed to press him to his breast in a close embrace, and

the cry rang clear '*Iqra!*' And so it happened these times; until
The first overpowering sensation yielded to a collected grasp of
the words which made clear his mission: its author, Allah, the
Creator; its subject, Man, Allah's wondrous handiwork . . .

And the instrument of that mission, the sanctified Pen, And
the sanctified Book, the Gift of Allah, Which men might read, or
write, or study, or treasure in their souls.

The veil was lifted from the Chosen One's eyes, And his
soul for a moment was filled with divine Ecstasy. . . . When this
passed, And he returned to the world of Time. . . . The darkness
now seemed tenfold dark; The solitude seemed tenfold empty;
The mount of Hira', henceforth known As the Mountain of Light,
the mere shell Of an intense memory. Was it a dream?

The lines above quoted from the introduction to the Koran before surah
1, outline the steps in the process which the Prophet went through to receive
his revelation. Some questions need to be carefully answered. What happened
to Muhammad in that cave? Was it internal or external to him? If it was a
dream, was that a product of his mind? If it was not a dream, did an entity
appear to him in the cave where he was meditating?

In either case, there are over a billion people who are following the
consciousness that enveloped him in that cave on Mount Hira. Are there any
special implications flowing from their faith to which the West should pay
attention? Through conjecture, can the identity of the angel that appeared to
Muhammad in that cave later be deduced?

It is certain from the early revelations onward that the entity that appeared
to the Prophet was not interested in teaching rational faith. It was
communicating a faith which cannot be explored or analyzed except through
'blind faith'. Many arguments within the words given by the angel *seem*
intuitively true if we accept the identity of the angel and the consciousness
he expressed. Later as the follower of Muhammad comes to believe these
propositions, *reality* becomes demonstratively true. A careful study of
Muhammad yields an interesting observation: it was the emotional experience
of being filled by the supernatural that became the confirmation for his
message.

When he started preaching in Mecca, many of his opponents accused
him of being possessed by the devil, *majnun* (surah 37:36;51:52). They titled
him a poet possessed and a sorcerer, or one possessed. His critics were silenced
by his gradual victories on the battlefield and by assasination. When his
opponents accused him of having produced the Koran himself, he put them
up to a challenge by asking them to produce ten surahs (surah 11:13). They

were given the freedom to call to their aid whomsoever they can, "other than Allah!"

The Koran became the lodestar for ascertaining the mantle of a true Prophet upon Muhammad, but that becomes the key weakness of the argument itself. The Koran attests the Prophet status; the Prophet attests the supernatural origin of Koran. There is a lack of an independent third element to verify either of these supporting claims. A truth-seeker is forced to ask how the Prophet could verify the identity of this angel who came to him at Mount Hira.

In fact the Koran also alludes to this in surah 17:88, "If the whole of mankind and Jinns were to gather together to produce the like of this Koran, they could not produce the like thereof, even if they backed up each other with help and support." From this passage, the possibility of evil spiritual beings, jinns, working with willing human agents to produce a similar work is raised as a challenge to the unbeliever. The pertinent question to ask is if that were to happen, how will such collusion be recognized by humanity?

The significant portion of the first epistle written by the Apostle John is dedicated to this question of recognizing which spirit comes from God and which voice is opposing the knowledge of God (I John 2:15-5:4). The three tests given in this passage are: (1) the confession about the identity of Jesus Christ (1 John 4:2), (2) the desire to resist sin (1 John 3:7-10) and (3) the desire to submit to or to oppose the authority of the church of God (1 John.4:6). The revelation that was given to the Prophet fails all three tests given in the Bible as demonstrated in this chapter and the next.

The wife of the Prophet was the first one who tried to console him after his chilling encounter with a supernatural being. Khadijah was certain that the encounter was divine and tried to wrap him with blankets to stop him from shivering. She was so convinced that his experience was no dream or delusion that she went to her cousin, Waraqah, an elderly back-slidden Christian, to verify her husband's experience. Waraqah confirmed that the Prophet's experience was from Allah and became a worshipper of Allah like other *hanifs*, Arab believers in the existence of only one unknown god. Later Khadijah, Ali, Abu Bakr, and Zayd joined the Prophet, bringing a woman, a child, a man of affairs, and a freedman into the worship of Allah demonstrating the equality of Islam (C.34 in the introduction to Koran). As in Christianity, the revelation of an angel produced a new community.

The church started with the coming of the Holy Spirit on the 120 followers of Jesus. The Muslim community started with the four people joining the Prophet. Unlike the early church these early converts did not know whom they were following because the angel did not appear to them. The Muslim community had to follow only the Prophet because they had no means to verify what the angel was telling him. The early church knew whom they were following because both leaders and followers were discipled by Jesus who made himself subject to the Old Testament scriptures and His heavenly Father.

For forty days the disciples of Jesus, both collectively and individually, were given the privilege of verifying in person the claim that He rose from the dead. If that were not sufficient, the experience of the cross was given as a legacy to the Christian to be experienced when they accept the claims of Jesus. The personal decision to follow Christ added the individual to a community of believers. It was in the context of this new community the scriptures became real to the new believer as they learned the meaning of the cross and started denying their self-directed walk.

Like Christ, the Prophet also was accused of being evil. He was called many things, including a soothsayer (surah 52:29, 69:42), a liar (38:4), and a sorcerer (51:39). The Prophet was accused of being led by a familiar spirit or even an evil spirit.

The experience of Christ, His temptations in the desert with the adversary offering Him the empires of this world, is credible because of His rejection of the offers coupled with the subsequent experience of the cross. Through these experiences He regained the title deed to the Earth and all the empires in it. The life of Christ, in the context of the larger canvas, cognitively adds up as verifiable logic even though it might not meet the standards of 'material science.' The questions raised about the character of the Prophet being led by a familiar spirit that was not necessarily good cannot be refuted unless the identity of the angel that appeared to him can be verified.

The entire revelation of the Koran hinges on the hidden personae that transmitted the revelation to Muhammad. Unfortunately some of the elements to verify this are not found in the Koran, so we have to rely on the hadith. We are told in the hadith that the revelations came to him in many forms including some very painful manifestations. According to this hadith, relayed by Ayesha, the child bride of the Prophet, even on a very cold day the Prophet would start sweating as the revelation came to him. If it came as a ringing of the bell, it was even more painful for the Prophet.

The Koran records that when the angel first came to him it was a frightening and unexpected experience (surah 96:1-5). It is believed that those five verses were the first direct revelation to the Prophet, and the rest of the verses in that same surah came after a break of time called *Fatrah*. This period was a time of confusion and fear in the life of the Prophet because he did not know the identity of this entity that kept appearing in his life.

Most Muslim scholars agree that surah 68, the next revelation that came to the Prophet, probably came after some months or even years. The remainder of unbelievers in surah 96, from verses 6-19, came after the *Fatrah,* the break. In surah 68:51-52, the revelation makes it plain that unbelievers will look at the followers of the Prophet, "when they hear the message and say surely he is possessed!"

The entity who taught the Prophet induced and expected an altered state of consciousness similar to being possessed. This matched the opinion of the people who did not believe the Prophet's message. It is noteworthy that in the last part of surah 96:13-18 there is a threat to anyone who turns away from the message of Allah, "we will call on the angels of punishment to deal with him." It is almost certain that fear and the experience of the supernatural played a major role in the development of this new altered state of consciousness. Fear became the backdrop for the Prophet and all the followers of Islam.

Though these surahs were given as the earliest verses, they are quietly tucked away towards the very end of the Koran which adds a sense of foreboding for those who reject the message of the Prophet. This sense of fear is assuaged only because Muslims believe the angel that appeared to the Prophet was Gabriel. He is mentioned by name in surahs 2:97-98 and 66:4, but most scholars also look at surahs 26:193 and 81:19-21 to identify Gabriel as the deliverer of Allah's message. How did the Prophet know his messenger was Gabriel?

If for arguments sake, we accept the claim that the angel who first appeared before the *Fatrah* was Gabriel, there is no assurance from the texts that the same angel reappeared later or that it was the Gabriel from heaven. Islamic scholars are mostly unanimous in stating that Gabriel appeared only twice in the visible form to the Prophet. The first was at the Mountain of Light when he was commanded with "Iqra" (C 29-35); the second time was at the ascension experience of his life (surah 17 introduction).

This second experience, a night journey from the Mosque in Mecca to the "Farthest Mosque" which Islamic scholars claimed to be in Jerusalem, was part of his journey to Allah's throne. To reach it he had to pass through the seven heavens. There are many Islamic scholars who argue that the entire experience was a vision while others believe that it was a literal physical journey. The possibility of deception becomes a serious concern when you try to ascertain the type of revelation this was and how the Prophet received his knowledge. The method of verification by which the angel Gabriel is identified is not clear in the Koran.

In the New Testament the angel Gabriel identifies himself first to Zachariah in Luke's account (Luke 1:19,26), and then Luke narrates that Gabriel was sent to Mary, the mother of Jesus. In the first encounter there is surprise on the part of the recipient of the message, but there is no fear or terror. Yet when Zachariah did not believe the message, the angel gave a clear sign by which he was not able to speak till his child, John the Baptist, was born. The element of the miraculous is used even in the Bible to confirm the claim of Gabriel.

In Daniel's account the angel Gabriel was asked by another being to explain the vision to Daniel. The background of this vision so terrified Daniel (Dan. 8:15-19) that the angel gave sleep to Daniel before he completed the task of teaching. In the second encounter although he was given the most amazing prophecy on the problem of evil, Daniel had no fear!

In the Biblical account of Gabriel's appearances there are no struggles similar to what the Prophet described. The angel that visited them comforts the recipients in the Bible. Why is there such a disparity between the experiences of the Prophet's visit and the angelic visits recorded in the Bible? Who was the angel that appeared to Muhammad?

As students of the Bible, we have no reason to believe that the angel visiting Muhammad was from the Kingdom of Light. This possibility of deception was anticipated by Apostle Paul. *But even if we, or an angel from heaven, preach any other gospel to you than what we have preached to you, let him be accursed* (Gal. 1:8).

In any case, the central argument of this chapter, could Muhammad have been deceived by a spiritual entity that used the name Gabriel, is secondary to the observation that Muhammad preached a different gospel. Muhammad's primary emotion was fear which allowed for most of the revelation to be given without any physical manifestation by this entity.

The Bible is certainly not always clear about the identities of the supernatural beings that came to the prophets in the Bible as seen in the experiences of Ezekiel and even in Daniel chapter 10. But these experiences are not the central thesis of the Bible. Life is viewed as a gift from God to be lived against the context of spiritual warfare.

The prophets of the Old Testament had a view that the God of Abraham, Isaac, and Jacob was at war with many gods who were limited in their ability except to cause fear in human beings. All of the prophets were unanimous that the God of the Bible was far more than all the other gods, and that He was involved in a rational plan to redeem the earth. It was this understanding that prompted Paul to affirm *For even if there are so-called gods, whether in heaven or on earth (as there are many gods and many lords), yet for us there is one God, the Father, of whom are all things, and we for Him; and one Lord Jesus Christ, through whom are all things, and through whom we live.* (1 Cor. 8:5-6).

To understand Islam it is essential to review the Bible's view of the role of evil and the purpose of God in the Genesis creation account as seen by the prophets Isaiah, Jeremiah, Job, Daniel, the Psalmists, and a host of New Testament authors.

We must conclude there is no way to ascertain who the angel was that visited Muhammad or if there really was an angel. The entire religion is based on the word of one man.

Would such testimony stand up in any court of law?

# The Origin of Evil

## Chapter Nine

*God asked Job, "Do you know the ordinances of the heavens? Can you set their dominion over the earth?"* (Job 38:33).

Every story worth telling has a hero and a villain, a central conflict between right and wrong, good and evil. The story of mankind is no different. Since the days when Adam and Eve strolled in the Garden of Eden, men and women have had to choose sides.

Unfortunately for us the sides are seldom clearly marked. The villain often masquerades as the hero, and the dark side of evil, the grotesque part we'd all recoil from is hidden behind something lovely, something good, something we're drawn to like romance, money, prestige, or a succulent piece of fruit. We're sucked in and suckered into believing evil is good and right is wrong.

How do we avoid such deception? We must know the players.

Who is the hero in our story? It is God of course.

Who is the villain? Satan, also known as Lucifer, *Iblis*, Leviathan, and the Devil is the villain. Naming him is the easy part. Recognizing him is much harder. Eve didn't recognize him when he came to her as a serpent in the garden.

Different religions have different theories about how the story will play out. Christianity teaches that Satan lost the battle at the cross and already is doomed for destruction. Islam warns followers about the tricks of Satan (*Iblis* in Arabic). But Islam differs from Judeo-Christian theology when it comes to the concept of original sin and the fall of humanity. In Islam Adam's sin does not affect the rest of humanity as Christianity teaches.

In the Old Testament *chattat* indicates sin against God (Lev. 5:1), a word that appears in the Koran, *khatia*, is in the context of a serious mistake (surah 33:5). The distinction between forgivable and unforgivable sins is also found in Islam, as it is in Christianity (I John 5:16), but each religion has its own list of unforgivable sins. In Islam, Allah's determining will dominates all other points of view regarding human responsibility.

Though the Koran states humans are responsible for their own actions, the predominant view in Islam is destiny, Allah's determining will. Surah 12:53 implies that human beings are capable of changing their ways with its opening phrase *"Although the human heart tends toward evil. . . ."* The human interaction with Allah is often a reciprocal give and take, but the emphasis is always on the sovereignty of Allah. In Islam Allah forgives the serious sins of those whom he will and likewise punishes for no sin those whom he will; he forgives and punishes according to his discretion. This sovereignty is grounded upon the fact that Allah has purchased the faithful, and they are his property (surah 9:111).

We do not find such discrimination in Christian theology. If we did, key verses would be radically different. For example, *For God so loved the world that he gave his only begotten son, that whosoever believeth in him should not perish but have everlasting life (John 3:16),* would read something like this: "For God so loved a few in the world that he gave his only begotten son so that some of those who believed in him should not perish." According to the Bible God does not play favorites. His love, faithfulness, and forgiveness are the things Christians know they can count on.

Islam views evil as flowing out of pride and self-determining arrogance which is pretty much how Christians see it too. The Islam example of evil behavior occurred when *Iblis*, Satan, refused to bow down before Adam as Allah commanded him to do. Satan is portrayed as a slightly noble entity because he will bow down only to Allah. Islamic theologians take the refusal of *Iblis* as a sign of his disobedience and pride (surah 2:34).

There are striking differences between the Biblical account and the Koranic account of the fall of Adam and Eve from their state of innocence. The Koran alleges that because Adam regretted his transgression, he was immediately forgiven by Allah (surah 2:36-39), and his fall brought only mortality to himself. Therefore his sin is treated as the sin of one individual thereby denying the concept of original sin. The Koran explicitly states man was created weak (surah 4:28). The person who belongs to Allah will receive the garden paradise as a reward if they fight for the cause of Allah. They are to be completely given over to Allah and must, if necessary, sacrifice their lives for him, slay and be slain.

Unlike the Koran, the Bible sets the spiritual narrative in the context of a conflict centered on evil, a war waged by the Kingdom of Light against the Kingdom of Darkness. In the Old Testament, the people of God are those who live in obedience to God and refrain from evil. In the New Testament the emphasis is on the gospel that liberates the individual. Each encourages man to live in voluntary obedience to God as father, not as a slave but as a free child of God. The God who presides over the Kingdom of Light is opposed by a host of other gods led by a fallen angel. Jews and Christians believe it is the God of Abraham, Isaac, and Jacob who presides over the Kingdom of Light.

Israel's history was set in the midst of many cultures that served other gods, but they were called to serve the true God. A force of evil opposed both Israel and their God. Many titles and word pictures are used to describe these dark forces and their leader. Both in the West and the East, in medicine, in religion, in folklore and tribal stories the symbol of the serpent is present as a depiction of evil.

An in-depth review of evil in the Bible gives logically reasonable answers to the problem of evil. They are centered on a very powerful angel in the heavenly realm, Lucifer, who is in total rebellion today. Though he was created good, he chose rebellion against God and became evil. The Bible does not describe the event in detail, but Lucifer is described as a powerful being who personally served God.

Satan was a model of perfection in both wisdom and beauty. He knew the unseen order in creation because of his proximity to God. He was able to hide his intentions from everyone's scrutiny except God. Since God honors the boundaries placed in his creation, we conclude that God did not use that knowledge of rebellion in Satan to destroy him completely. God has been using this rebel to accomplish higher purposes.

Just as God is truth and his beauty resides in his absence of deceit, Satan's sting is in his ability to deceive and hide his motives. Because God has not revealed everything to man yet, Satan is able to create doubt about God's character. His primary *modus operandi* is through casting aspersions on God's character, and to do that effectively he hides from human experience.

The God of the Bible insists that we seek Him and He hides until we do. Even after we start seeking Him, He reveals himself in a progressive fashion.

Hebrews 11:6 states: *he who comes to God must believe that He is, and that He is a rewarder of those who diligently seek Him.*

The reward that God gives the seeker is the revelation of Himself and the privilege of knowing Him and having eternal life in Christ. If a revelation of God is not followed up with obedience, then God will have to honor His law by judging the person who chose not to obey.

It is worth noting that Satan hides too but for very different reasons. In one sense even in hiding Satan is copying God, the father of all creation. But Satan's perverse goal in hiding is to encourage the idea that he does not exist. Deception, his greatest weapon, was the guise that enabled him to make the heavenly appeal to a third of the angels to doubt the character of God. Satan has hid his character from all of his followers as well, but he is unable to hide it from God.

Satan's goal is to prevent men and women from reaching their destiny with God because that would begin his imprisonment. The destiny of mankind, as defined by Augustine, is to develop character and grow in the knowledge of God until man is ready to dwell with Him in the City of God. Satan will be imprisoned before the "City of God" is inaugurated.

It is interesting to note when we look in the Bible, we do not find Satan coming to tempt every one. He made only two appearances to tempt. It was the first Adam in the Garden of Eden and then the last Adam, Jesus Christ in the desert. In both of these temptations two types of destiny were at stake for mankind. With the first Adam, Satan hid behind the created animal, the serpent. With the second Adam, he could not hide. When Jesus fasted, he gave up his human energy and vigor. When the first Adam was tempted, he was completely satiated with all the fruits in the garden. In such a state of prosperity Satan did not have to reveal himself. He hid in the form of the serpent. Had he come revealing himself there would have been no temptation for the first Adam would have rejected Satan's offer. The power of temptation lies in the half-truths present in the temptation.

If we study Luke's and Matthew's narrations, we find subtle differences. Luke writes, *Jesus . . . being tempted for forty days by the devil. And in those days He ate nothing, and afterward, when they had ended, He was hungry. And the devil said to Him, "If You are the Son of God, command this stone to become bread"* (Lk. 4:2-3).

Matthew states it from a different perspective. *And when He had fasted forty days and forty nights, afterward He was hungry. Now when the tempter came to Him, he said, "If You are the Son of God, command that these stones become bread"* (Mt. 4:2-3).

These differences illustrate a very important truth. Satan will hide as much as possible, and it is only when there is no alternative left for him to continue his temptations that he is forced to reveal himself. If Jesus had not persisted in fasting all those days, there is every reason to believe that Satan would not have been forced to reveal himself. As Matthew subtly points out, at the end of 40 days the tempter *came to Jesus*. Throughout the 40 days of the fast, Satan was obviously able to tempt Jesus by hiding behind a facade. It is because of this principle Jesus stated, *"This kind can come out by nothing but prayer and fasting"*(Mk. 9:29).

The writers in the Bible unanimously agree that Jesus came to restore mankind to God by defeating Satan through revealing his deception and destroying his power. Luke closes this section on temptation by stating, *When the devil had finished all this tempting, he left him until an opportune time* (Lk 4:13). The opportune time came at the cross. The cross of Christ was the intersection point between the first prototype of the nation-state, Israel, and the longest lasting human empire, the Roman Empire.

Satan was able to prevent the development of a citizenry educated in the law in Israel by tempting the people to follow the practices of the neighboring nations. Rome was the embodiment of those practices: a powerful army, a pantheon of gods, and unbridled power for their Caesar. The nation Israel was repeatedly warned by God not to follow the practice of having a king like the neighboring nations. But Satan was able to entice the Jewish nation to follow the wicked gods of the neighboring nations, which in turn corrupted the entire nation of Israel. Finally against God's desire, when Israel insisted on a king, God granted it to them. After that Satan was able to delay God's plan for Israel. This caused Satan to believe that he would be able to do the same to God at Calvary. But unlike the disobedient Israelites earlier, Satan had to deal then with an obedient Jesus.

When the Jewish leaders cried to the Roman rulers for the crucifixion of Jesus, Satan must have thought he had again thwarted God's plan for mankind. But God allowed Satan to deceive himself in his self-absorption. In all of his deception Satan thought he and his rulers were planning the death of Jesus when in actuality Jesus carefully fulfilled the Scripture by planning every step of his passion. If Satan had fooled anyone, he only fooled himself at the cross.

F. J. Huegel writes in *That old Serpent, the Devil*: "In the desperate conflict Christ waged, in which He lost His life, was He mistaken? Was it really the prince of this world He had to face — a terrible supernatural being whose hate for God was as dark and as deep as hell? Or was he deluded?"

Jesus clearly stated that he is inaugurating the Kingdom of God. John the beloved writes, *For this purpose the Son of God was manifested, that He might destroy the works of the devil* (1 Jn. 3:8). In the inauguration of the Kingdom and proclaiming the era of Jubilee, Jesus explicitly initiated the destruction of the power structure behind the Kingdom of Darkness.

Satan's main characteristic, as the Bible points out, is his total preoccupation with himself. Satan is described as having made five "I will" statements. All the "I will" statements  centered around the goal of making himself like the Most High God. Satan states: *"I will ascend into heaven, I will exalt my throne above the stars of God; I will also sit on the mount of the congregation On the farthest sides of the north; I will ascend above the heights of the clouds, I will be like the Most High"* (Isa. 14:13-14). Equality or even ascendancy over God seems to be his primary motive.

From the time Satan made his first "I will" statement, there has been progressive degeneration because of the selfishness in Satan and in his sphere of influence. The hideousness of total preoccupation with one's own self is detestable even to wicked human beings. Therefore Satan cannot reveal himself to his followers even when they want to join him in opposing God and His plan. Just as God is transparent and revels in revealing himself in such awe-inspiring humility, Satan hides because of his total pride. He is too proud to show others how detestable he is and too vengeful to admit his error of rebellion.

This reality which prompted Satan's total preoccupation with himself makes him an entity with which meaningful relationship is impossible. The five pillars of Islam are reflections of these dominant passions in Satan. It is in the fifth pillar, the Hajj, that he receives worship from deceived human beings. The personalities suffer deterioration in a progressive manner as they follow this path of worship. Satan, too, had a similar story.

Ezekiel writes about Satan's fall. *"Your heart was lifted up because of your beauty; You corrupted your wisdom for the sake of your splendor; I cast you to the ground, I laid you before kings, That they might gaze at you* (Ezek. 28:17). There was a time when Satan was the paragon of virtues like wisdom and splendor. But the calcification of his persona started with pride, the root of all sin. Then he enticed other entities to join his rebellion; a third of the angelic hosts were under his influence (Rev.12:4).

When Paul talks about Jesus' crucifixion, he refers to rulers of this age, *none of the rulers of this age knew; for had they known, they would not have crucified the Lord of glory* (1 Cor. 2:8). These rulers are listed by the great prophet Isaiah from chapter 8 through 35. The ruling entities over the ancient nations of Assyria (Turkey), Babylon (Iraq), Philistine (Palestine), Moab and Edom (Jordan), Damascus (Syria), Cush (Ethiopia), Egypt, Tyre (Lebanon) and others is a comprehensive list of the nations around Israel. All the human kingdoms and nations are controlled by powerful angels that are part of the Kingdom of Darkness in Satan's hierarchy (Dan. 10:13,20).

The Bible describes Satan with many titles that are very revealing. Satan is described as an adversary, (1 Kings 11:14,23; 1 Thess. 2:18) showing him as an opposing force in human affairs. Devil, meaning a hairy goat (Isa. 13:21, 34:14) reveals an animalistic nature, an inability to keep the law. The Greek term diabolos, slanderer or accuser, is used more than thirty times in the New Testament. Gossip, slandering, and libel are to be viewed as deadly habits initiated by Satan. Beelzebub, God of the Philistines (2 Kings 1:2,16), the Serpent (Rev.12:9, Isa. 27:1, 2 Cor. 11:3), Roaring Lion (1 Pet. 5:8), Liar (Jn. 8:44), the Tempter (Mt. 4:3), the Dragon (Rev. 12:3,7,8), the evil one (1 Jn. 5:19) are all different titles given to Satan in the Bible. Many of the descriptions of Satan are related to the animal kingdom, but the Bible insists that humanity was created in the image of God.

The philosophical systems of the world will accept that there is potential for evil in man. Often they want to describe that as the process of learning that men have to go through to understand the meaning of life. Some systems like Hinduism call it ignorance in man. Islam makes the claim there is no original sin in the universe. Both religions exclude the sins of self-righteousness which are seen more clearly by the humble. Only the Bible makes the claim that man feels guilty because there is true moral guilt in man.

The Bible identifies the error of other systems of thinking when they try to make evil an abstract concept. The Bible declares there is no evil in this world without an agent: No murder without a murderer! No adultery without adulterers! No lies without a liar. When there is evil, there is an agent, a perpetrator.

Jesus made it very clear that Satan was the primary agent of evil in the universe. People who do not acknowledge their natural inclination towards selfish-fulfillment as sin are the secondary agents. How did Jesus portray the interaction between the primary agent of evil, Satan, and people? In the parable of the sower (Mt. 13:19) Jesus tells us clearly the 'evil one' came and snatched away the sown seed (Word of God). The use of the phrase 'evil one' pointed to Satan. Not allowing the message of the Bible to take root in a person's life is portrayed as the work of Satan. Paul states that same principle in, *it is veiled to those who are perishing, whose minds the god of this age has blinded, who do not believe, lest the light of the gospel of the glory of Christ, who is the image of God, should shine on them* (2 Cor. 4:3-4).

Satan is personally held responsible for the *closing of the minds* of people and the *guarding of the minds* of the people against truth. Isaiah called this closing of the mind as a shroud or veil at the systemic level. At an individual level this behavior leads to personal death, but at an aggregate level or systemic level this closing of the minds creates a system that rejects truth.

According to Jesus, truth or the search for truth is alien to Satan, his followers, and the systems controlled by him. Jesus identified Satan and declared that he *does not stand in the truth, because there is no truth in him. When he speaks a lie, he speaks from his own resources, for he is a liar and the father of it* (Jn. 8:44).

It is tragic today that the church does not engage the secular mind in the contradictions that exist in the Islamic system of thinking with respect to evil and its origin. Only the Bible looks at the evil and clearly points out the seeming irrationality behind the evil and fiendish events of this world. The axiomatic proclamations of the Bible about Satan and the domain of evil can very reasonably be verified in the events of modern times. But the church has not sufficiently expounded the Bible to bring this to attention.

The divine revelation in the Scriptures provides a reliable source of categories about reality. But autonomous man would like to deny it. Biblical categories are all the more applicable when it comes to the realm of the invisible. Where the Bible is silent or leaves room for ambiguity the expositor has to be careful. Like most scientific knowledge, through hypothesis testing, using observations and empirical data, Biblical reality is verifiable. Where the Bible has spoken clearly we do not have to be tentative. But in understanding the scripture we need to use biblical reasoning.

Biblical reasoning will not violate the hierarchy of logical reasoning because logical reasoning is just a subset of biblical reasoning. Biblical reasoning in addition to logical reasoning contains truth through revelation. What sets apart this Biblical revelation is the fact that it is verifiable. The Bible seems to clearly indicate that this also applies to the personhood, character, and activities of Satan.

There is no such reasoning in Islam.

# Humanity's Response to Evil

## Chapter Ten

It is an undeniable fact that evil exists in the world, and the Bible makes it clear who is responsible for the treachery with which we must cope. Three titles given to Satan reveal the extensive scope of the unseen satanic powers fighting against us.

As the *god of this world,* and *prince of the power of the air* Satan dominates the world from the atmosphere. These two titles, given to him identifying him as the force behind the kingdoms of this earth, disclose the unseen normal flow of human history as it occurs in the Kingdom of Darkness. The Apostle Paul cautioned that *we do not wrestle against flesh and blood, but against principalities, against powers, against the rulers of the darkness of this age, against spiritual hosts of wickedness in the heavenly places* (Eph. 6:12).

In a third view of Satan from the Bible he disguises himself as *an angel of light* (2 Cor. 11:14). It is this side, the beautiful side of evil, that confuses most human beings. Because deception is one of Satan's strongest weapons he uses it most effectively in making bad things look so enticing, so right. Human selfishness is one of his triumphs for it seems so logical to look out for one's rights to ensure self-preservation. Nazism, communism, non-Christian religions (self-centered righteousness), and the large organizations that control human systems seem to be rooted in human selfishness. This selfishness exemplified by leadership is only a reflection of the human heart.

Evil is mind-numbing and senseless. But the Bible does not trivialize it by trying to give it a philosophical explanation. No system of thought has provided logical and verifiable reasons for the problem of evil other than the Bible. Rational answers might be emotionally satisfying, but they eventually take the focus away from the key objective, the elimination of evil.

According to the Bible, God pronounced judgment on Satan by using the seed of the woman, Jesus Christ, to crush his head. Therefore Satan has directed his hatred against women, hoping to crush them, the progenitor of the seed. Ever since Christ's death on Calvary, every woman reminds Satan of his inevitable day of judgment by God. This is a reality that Amartya Sen, Nobel laureate in economics, verified proving that whenever major crises occur, the population of women has decreased. Famines and other catastrophic events can be a consequence of the conflict in the unseen world. Satan is able to direct his wrath specifically against women during such crises. But during the periods of peace or regular flow of history, Satan expresses his anger towards women through men who are possessed by him and through religions, such as Islam, that are repressive to women.

The ability to procreate makes human beings a superior species to the fallen angelic order. The Bible states explicitly there is no procreative ability in the angelic order. Modern culture, dominated by Satan, has no awe for the sacredness of human sexuality. In Islamic nations, to maintain political control, Satan encourages a system of sexual repression which allows him to keep the Muslims loyal to him through power. The debauchery projected by the Western media is used by Islamists to convince the moderate Muslim to support their political repression within their Islamic nation-states.

Through rebellion, Satan is able to keep deep anger burning in human hearts against God the Father. Satan knows the power, the purity, and the immovable character of God. This purity enrages Satan and his anger is manifested through human beings who have not yielded their will to God and therefore are serving evil. In Islam the idea of Allah as father of all spirits is one of the least acceptable tenets in their theology.

Even though human history seems to lack any cohesion in development or a focus, the Bible insists that history is purposefully progressing towards certain events. Human beings have been given the ability to choose God's will or self-will. If self-will is chosen, that choice will be in the context of the larger system, human history, which is under the control of Satan because of Adam's fall. Ever since that event, all human systems have intentionally or unintentionally served the god of this world, Satan.

Judaism, the earliest religion to develop an all-pervading sense of the holiness and righteousness of God, puts great emphasis on personal repentance and seeking after God. Like Buddhism, the primary focus in Judaism is on the human response to the demands of a personal god. Unlike Buddhism, God is a revealed entity in the Hebrew Bible. This in turn demands a response from the Jew. The Psalms capture the agony of a Jewish believer in the face of suffering and human wickedness.

The major contribution of Judaism is the universal concept of the law revealed through the prophet Moses, the ethical demands of living within agreed upon boundaries of a society. The emphasis has always been in waiting for the redeemer God, Jehovah (Yahweh), who carved a nation for himself, the Jewish people through Moses. Israel was the only nation that was formed in the ancient world as a response to their God. This explains the ability of the modern Jew, in spite of all of the subjection of the Jewish people to unparalleled wickedness in the twentieth century, to view the formation of the state of Israel as a gift from Yahweh.

In spite of the mention of the human fall in Genesis through the serpent and the trial of Job by Satan, Judaism in practice is a religion without an action plan against Satan, the agent of evil. In that sense, Judaism is a very passive religion with great emphasis on the law and the rational approach in learning and applying the law. Judaism laid the foundation for the central theme of Christianity, Jesus Christ undoing the works of evil perpetrated on humanity by Satan. Satan briefly appears in the prologue of Genesis and is also mentioned sporadically in the other books. But he is first pictured in Job as a respectable figure commissioned with the task of testing the faithful people on earth. It was Christ who drew out Satan's true colors, especially after the temptation story.

Islam, the youngest of the three absolutist religions, has a cosmology in which Allah created the world in six days. Beside himself there are only two other uncreated beings: (1) the prototype of the Koran, "mother of the Book" and (2) the throne (*Khursi*) upon which Allah is seated in the seventh heaven surrounded by angels, pure and sexless beings. Islam also teaches the fall of Adam was the work of Satan. Men are separated from the angels by the jinn, male and female inhabitants of the desert, created from smokeless fire. The lowest of creation in Allah's estate is the devil or Satan. He was an angel at one time but was expelled from heaven for refusing to bow down to Adam at Allah's command. To the Sufi Muslim, Satan was nobler than man because he was willing to risk expulsion from heaven by refusing to worship someone other than Allah. After all Adam was only a creation of Allah.

Standard Muslim polemics would state that Islam, like Judaism, has no concept of original sin that stems from man. Man is born in purity or *fitrah*. The Koran offers by way of insistent warning and wise guidance a way of liberation from ignorance and barbarism. Called *jahiliya* in the Arabic of the Koran, sin in man is expelled through the progressive interiorization of the word of Allah. So evil in Islam is external to Islam; evil is attributed to the unbelievers. In many senses the figure of Satan is a confusing symbol in Islam which gives no coherent explanation to the problem of evil.

Christianity is at the other end of the spectrum of religions in its attempt to explain wickedness and suffering. In Christianity the two issues are closely related, almost intertwined. Christianity's two extreme responses to suffering were well expressed by two 19th century Russian novelists, Leo Tolstoy and Fyodor Dostoevsky. Tolstoy was a great intellectual fascinated by the Bible and the absoluteness of God's character as revealed in the life of Jesus. He wrote with penetrating passion on the character of God and the character of man. In redemption, Christ saves human beings from the evil overlord, Satan, and then transforms them to His likeness.

For Dostoevsky the problem of suffering was beyond comprehension. He shares his struggle in accepting God's design of this world with all of its terrible wickedness and suffering. In the words of one of his characters, "I recognize in all humility that I cannot understand why the world is arranged as it is."

But the Christian does not have all the facts about the universe as God knows it. There is a set of intelligent answers given to this question in the Bible. The Bible insists that the answers are both true and reasonable. The tragedy of human sin predicated on Satan's offer, empowered by human consent, reveals the boundless love of God at Calvary. The Bible insists that the wrongs of life would be totally eradicated by an act of sovereign re-creation in the fullness of time when time would come to an end. But the external act of re-creation would start with the binding and punishing of Satan, the agent of evil and the author of human suffering, even as the internal re-creation of the believers is now being accomplished through sanctification.

Unfortunately modern Christian theology looks at the demonology presented in the Bible with great skepticism. The view that the devil and evil spirits are mythological characters, based on the cultural and belief framework of thousands of years ago, seems to be more acceptable among some modern Western Christians. The fact that Ed Kemper, Ted Bundy, and Jeffrey Dahmer demonstrated characteristics of being possessed by an inordinate consciousness that was trying to possess their victims seem to validate the Biblical view. But a central piece of the argument is in the parallels between the lives of Josef Stalin, Adolf Hitler, and Satan as described in the Bible.

Dostoevsky presents two problems regarding evil: first the limitless vulgarity, the monotonous repetition of senseless cruelty towards fellow human beings, making evil very banal and senseless. This forced modern writers like Hannah Arendt to coin the phrase like 'banality of evil'. This problem violates the sense of emotional well-being. The second problem that Dostoevsky poses is the difficulty for human beings to accept an all-powerful God permitting such cruelty. This second problem is a problem of reason. Confronting the cause of evil, the Bible, with a well laid out approach, states that its reasoning is verifiable in human experience.

As today's largest human systems, nation-states and their behavior can be correlated to the understanding of evil shared by the majority which comes from the religious faith of the majority or an influential minority with power. An example from history for the latter is the reluctant realization in Britain of the need to fight Germany at any cost during the height of Nazi aggression in 1939.

Thomas Sowell writes in *The Quest for Cosmic Justice* (p. 114).

> Yet, at the time, little of this was understood in the West beyond the ranks of a very few like Winston Churchill, who was then a back bencher in Parliament, alienated from his own party and often an object of disdain and ridicule, when he was noticed at all. By contrast, when Chamberlain prepared to fly to Munich for his historic meeting with Hitler in 1938, he left amid tumultuous cheers and applause and the virtually unanimous support of all parties in the House of Commons, and was similarly welcomed back with great acclaim in Parliament and in the country, as he proclaimed "peace in our time." For all practical purposes it seemed suicidal for Britain to fight the Nazi war machine, especially when Hitler was willing to make peace with a Britain without Churchill. But a definitive minority believed that Nazism was evil and vowed to strengthen the national resolve.

The frequency of genocide starting with the Armenians by the Turks at the beginning of the twentieth century, Nanking by the Japanese, Jews and Gypsies by Nazi Germany, Hindus in Pakistan, Muslims in India, Hutus and Tutsis in Rwanda, the educated in Cambodia by Polpot, and Bosnians in Yugoslavia all defy ordinary explanations. Yet few modern systems of philosophy want to give any place to the Satan of Scripture or the power structure that he controlled in history.

George Otis Jr. in his book, *The Last of the Giants,* states the differences between God's authority and Satan's authority on earth. "While God is the rightful head of human families (*ethnos* - tribes and people groups), Satan is in general control over human systems (*kosmos* - kingdoms and structures). Whereas God's authority is derived through fatherhood, Satan's rule is achieved through the *volition of men.*" He goes on to state, "Satan has done a masterful job of empowering "the peddlers of political dreams" from Hitler's Goebbels to Mao's Red Guards to enslave the masses." He rightfully seems to believe that the rest of the world would eventually copy the New World Order, the utopia peddled by the intellectuals in the West, when Europe establishes and promotes it.

If Hitler's character and life is analyzed against the backdrop of the Biblical information on Satan in this chapter, his shadowy force in history becomes more exposed. Then history itself will make more sense as Augustine tried to demonstrate. Hitler indeed was acting out a script put together for him from long back, especially after he crossed certain God-ordained boundaries. This seemed to have taken place several times in his life such as the spiritual experience he had while in the hospital. This vision was the call of Satan.

When Hitler responded to that call he crossed a spiritual boundary. Satan's goal was to gain more time in his losing battle against Jesus Christ, the lion of Judah, the Jewish messiah still rejected by the Jewish nation. As European Jewry was central to the formation of the Jewish nation, their total elimination would have been the end of God's redemptive plan. Hitler was awakened in his spirituality long before this event as evidenced by the voice that guided him through World War I.

As attested to later by his fellow soldiers, Hitler sensed the invisible foes of the German people, offering further evidence that he was indeed a spiritually awakened man or a medium. This would also explain Hitler being labeled as the 'Medicine man' by Carl Jung as well as his hypnotic persuasiveness as felt by Albert Speer. Hitler crossed a spiritual boundary another time. Upon the death of Geli Rubel he decided to become a vegetarian which was more of an act of consecration to the service of his master, Wotan, than a dietary decision.

Satan knows the power and immovable character of God. This enrages Satan and his anger is made manifest in human beings who have yielded their will in serving evil. Authority figures, both God the Father and human fathers, put boundaries to personality. People who find it impossible to accept these limits on their personality destroy their own lives and those of others. The examples in this chapter violated their own boundaries as well as those of others. All of them carried deep rooted anger against the father figure in their lives. Unlike Hitler, the anger of others were directed against women which again fits the Biblical description of Satan and the human fall in Genesis.

To understand Hitler's anger toward the Jewish people we need to understand how the Bible views Satan's work in the nation-states. The Bible explains how Satan works in a large system like a society or nation-state and a character sketch of Satan can be cobbled together from the above descriptions in any large system like a nation-state or a community.

Jesus said that truth or the search for truth is alien to Satan, his followers, and the systems controlled by him. But then Satan's story is often a story of "almost" because in the end Jesus Christ, the Lion of Judah, brings back mankind and the creation into the relationship with God that was in the original intent. Therefore evil shall not triumph though it causes great damage. It will be wiped out by good.

Light always overcomes darkness. The question for every person to answer is this: "Will I chose to be a part of the light?"

# Islam's Conflict with the West

# Abraham, Patriarch of Three Religions

## Chapter 11

Abraham, the archetypal symbol of the follower of God in Judaism, Christianity, and Islam, is recognized as a historical figure even by secular scholars. However it is hard to distinguish which stories narrated in the three traditions can be treated as history. To understand the enduring conflict in the Middle East it is essential to start with Abraham.

Judeo-Christian tradition essentially agrees on all the stories of Abraham in the Torah, even though their interpretations differ. In the Islamic tradition even the stories on Abraham differ because of emphasis given to the minor characters in the Torah narrative. The early traditions of Islam were in agreement with the Judeo-Christian narrative which depicted Isaac as the son offered by Abraham for sacrifice, but today all Islamic scholars view Ishmael as the son offered by Abraham. This change of perspective is not unique to Islamic scholars.

Within the framework of these three major faiths there are myriad pictures of Abraham, many incompatible with one another. The two extreme perspectives among Western scholars on Abraham make him into a bipolar personality. One treats the narrative as a myth built by the critical Jewish and Christian scholars; the other position is taken by scholars like William Albright. In 1949 after years of pains-taking study Albright declared, "There can be little doubt about the substantial historicity of the patriarchal narratives." Though the historicity of Abraham cannot be proven, to almost three billion people who trace their faith to Abraham, he is either the first Jew or the first Muslim, based on the believers' persuasion.

The facts central to all three religions that are deemed true about Abraham are his nomadic life-style, a radical departure from the existing traditions of society, a monotheistic pursuit of God, a covenant, a sacrifice, and an acceptance by God. When Abraham left Ur of the Chaldeans, he left his family, traditions, and the safety of a settled life in an advanced city to follow the voice of God. Abram, as he was known then, became a semi-nomad, commonly known as *Aramu* or *Arabu*, the precursor to the better-known word Arab.

With great care the Judeo-Christian narrative calls him an Aramean, a nomad. The Koran largely ignores Abraham's conscious choice of a nomadic life style. In the Koran "Abraham was not a Jew nor yet a Christian; But he was true in Faith, And bowed his will to Allah's (which is to Islam), And he joined not gods with Allah"(surah 3:67). The great virtue of Abraham, as depicted in the Koran, was not his friendship with God but his surrender to Allah's will.

It is true the Koran calls Abraham a friend of God, to be precise *Khalil Allah*, Friend of Allah (surah 4:125), but the friendship is between a creator and the creation, a teacher and a student, a master and a servant. It is not considered an evolving friendship but a contractual agreement. So the great call of the Koran, to submit to Allah like Abraham and Muhammad, is to obey without question by following Abraham's example like Muhammad did (surah 3:68). Abraham is called an *ummah*, a model, a paragon of piety (surah 16:120-123) where he remained true in faith to Allah without joining other gods with Allah. The distinct command is "Follow the ways of Abraham, The True in Faith, and he Joined not gods with Allah."

Islam, built on the didactic approach of the Koran, presents the life of Abraham almost picture perfect for instruction with little narrative. In the sixth surah Abraham challenges his father about the idols present in his family. Yet Abraham's response to idolatry is revealed only in the twenty-first surah. He was reported to have broken the smaller idols around the larger idol, and when he was questioned, he told his interrogators to ask the chief idol . . . if it could speak.

In the Koran Abraham, the young logician, reveals perfection as he faces the test of fire. An aura of perfect obedience is accorded to Abraham even in his childhood. In these narratives, Islam emphasizes the childhood of Abraham which is completely ignored in the Bible. Judaism with its rich emphasis on story telling is totally silent about Abraham's childhood. In fact the Biblical narrative about Abraham starts with the death of his father, Terah.

At the beginning God's demands on Abraham appeared minimal. He had only to leave his home and his people. But for an aging man of great wealth, with no children, living at the edge of a desert, it practically meant total surrender to a voice that spoke of an unknown destiny. He was only told 'to go to a land that I will show you'. It was in meeting this minimal demand, that Abraham demonstrated the life of total surrender to a God who does not give a name or a definite destination. Trusting this voice he left a life of certainty to live a life of uncertainty in the barren desert against the howling winds. He did this to gain an understanding of the God he was trying to know.

In the Torah, as Abraham's friendship with God increases, God changed his name from Abram to Abraham. He was promised a child at the beginning of his journey, but he wandered for almost ten years as a restless nomad, a precursor to the Bedouin and the Pilgrim. He and his wife, Sarah, had been unable to procreate on their own. Even though Abraham trusted God unconditionally to give him a child (Gen. 15:6) when Sarah brought Hagar to him as a concubine, he accepted her suggestion without questioning. At eighty-six Abraham had his first-born son, Ishmael, though not through his wife, Sarah. Ishmael's birth made Sarah jealous, and her harsh treatment eventually caused Hagar to run away.

The most amazing passage in this narrative is the appearance of the Angel of the Lord to Hagar recorded in Genesis 16 and later in Genesis 21. It almost appears that God is working on both sides of the fence with Abraham and Sarah on one side and Hagar and Ishmael on the other. This perspective is missing in the Koran.

God allowed Abraham to enjoy Ishmael, the child of his flesh, for thirteen years. In the meantime Abraham learned to converse with God, and he confessed that before Ishmael was born he was fearful of not having children. Now Abraham wanted God to bless Ishmael.

God made a covenant with Abraham with an elaborate ritual. Almost thirteen years after Ishmael's birth God insisted on adding a physical sign to his covenant. For using his manhood according to Sarah's advice, God now demands a permanent sign as a reminder to Abram to dedicate his reproductive ability to God. God's invasion of the most private areas of Abraham's life is complemented by another astounding demand. God turned his attention to Abraham's most public possession, his name. Then both he and his wife had their names changed. They became Abraham and Sarah in their long trek with God and towards God.

The biggest test of Abraham's life comes in chapter 22 of Genesis where he is asked by God to sacrifice his son of promise, Isaac. It is impossible to comprehend the impact on Abraham and Sarah, though nothing is mentioned about her reaction. The miracle child, the child of promise, was now to be given as a human sacrifice to the God he thought was his friend.

In this dramatic story Abraham went on a three-day journey with his son, Isaac, and two servants, to a specially selected mountain in the land of Moriah, modern Jerusalem. Abraham, believing that his friend, God, had a plan, took Isaac alone to the sacrifice. When God dramatically provided a ram just before Abraham completed the sacrifice, two things were confirmed: (1) Abraham's character, "..for now I know that you fear God, since you have not withheld your son, your only son, from Me," and (2) God is a provider beyond human understanding. Abraham named him, Yaweh Yireh. Only a dear friend gives a special name to a true friend! In Jewish understanding through *akedah*, the binding of Isaac, Abraham demonstrated to God his supreme obedience by his willingness to sacrifice Isaac who was dearer to Abraham than his own life.

Even though the Koran is not clear, most Islamic scholars reject the Biblical notion of Abraham's willingness to sacrifice Isaac. Islamic scholars now insist that Ishmael was the son Abraham offered for sacrifice, though Ishmael is only mentioned twelve times in the Koran. Surah 19 calls Ishmael "a man of his word, an apostle, and a prophet. He enjoined prayer and almsgiving on his people and his Lord was pleased with him." When he is mentioned in surah 19, he follows Aaron, the brother of Moses who came in history five hundred years after Ishmael. What is Ishmael's role in revealing the character of Allah other than the fact that he is the progenitor of Muhammed?

It is almost certain that Abraham believed in life after death. He either expected God to bring Isaac back to life or expected to join Isaac and God after his own death. In any case two aspects of this story are accepted by all three traditions: (1) Abraham's belief in the unseen God, and (2) Isaac, as a young man, was not oblivious to these events. Did he share in his father's faith of eternity prior to this event?

From Abraham onwards there would be three groups of people: those called by God, those who call on God, and those who reject God. Even the called people have the freedom to reject the call as the long history of friendship with God reveals!

In the Koran, the Jews are accused of covering up the Muslim character of Abraham's faith in God (surahs 2:140, 2:135, 3:65-67). But a careful study of the Koran reveals that Allah's true character is covered up, and the student is left with a master who is beyond the relational. The Koran states that Allah is faithful to his servants, not as a friend but as a master. Abraham, Lot, and Noah, (surah 21:51-77) were aided by Allah because they supported the cause of Allah (surah 47:7).

**Abraham and the Surahs:**

Out of the twenty-five prophets in Islam, eighteen come from Abraham's family. His complete devotion to Allah in the face of overwhelming odds separated Abraham to Allah. The example in surah 2, where Allah provides Abraham with proof of His ability to bring the dead back to life and his conversing with Allah only confirms the superior/subordinate relationship in the Koran. This pattern is embedded in the Koran because there is no third-person narrative in it. Allah speaks directly in all six thousand two hundred plus verses of the Koran.

Abraham is mentioned in 25 of the 114 surahs in the Koran with surah 14 named after him. The universality of Islam is captured by Abraham even while the particulars seem error-filled compared to the earlier revealed scriptures. In surah.2:130-132, the legacy of faith, was given to Abraham and his sons, especially Jacob, the son of Isaac. But Abraham did not pass his legacy of faith to Ishmael according to the Bible. Nevertheless the Koran adds Ishmael to the phrase God of Abraham, Isaac, and Jacob.

The most important characteristic of Abraham in the Koran is his extreme rejection of idolatry (surah 60) while affirming monotheism. In the rejection of idolatry the faith of Abraham goes through a radical change in Islam.

Though surah 14 is named after *Ibrahim* (Abraham), it follows surah 10 for *Yunus* (Jonah), and surah 12 for *Yusuf* (Joseph), his great grandson. Thus the Koran does not follow a chronological order. According to surah 2 Islam predated Abraham. It is *also* important to note that in surah 29:27 the role of prophecy was given to the line of Abraham, Isaac, and Jacob, not to the progeny through Ishmael as taught in Islam.

All three traditions agree that Abraham was following the one and only God of the universe. But the Koran claims that Allah and God are one (surah 29:47-29). The mystery of the name of God, a point of fundamental difference between the three traditions, especially between Islam and the other two, starts with the life of Abraham. If the three traditions were to find peace among them, it is important that they go back to the figure of Abraham and start from him. The only universality that exists among the three traditions comes from Abraham. He is devout, dedicated, deductive, and as a destroyer of traditions is willing to discard his wrong notions of God for the divine message.

Since this man is worthy of God, an attempt for the universal should start with this man. In the selection of Abraham, God divides humanity into two groups: the followers of Abraham and the others. But as the historical narrative progresses, the followers of Abraham fall into three major traditions with multiple divisions in each tradition. All three agree that Abraham believed in one God who was invisible, a tradition without either gods or idols.

Abraham was the true transitional figure from a polytheist to a monotheist. God was the voice that asked him to make the journey. Each tradition differs on the nature of this unseen voice, yet all agree on Abraham's commitment to make the journey in total obedience and surrender. Abraham is the classic suitor who proves his love through his deeds, not to a fiancée but to the creator of the universe! But in later narratives, the roles are reversed in Judaism as God becomes the suitor and Abraham becomes the wooed. This view of love between a wooer and his maid existing between God and humanity is scandalous to a Muslim and never found in the Koran. Yet Abraham, the first monotheist, lived the life of a devotee by abandoning himself to a single relationship to his God like a *monogamist.*

Did God need a new type of believer after the disaster of Noah? God needed somebody who would need Him in order to meet God's standards. Abraham was that person. Islam would like us to believe Muhammad looked like that person, but he was far different from Abraham. Islam's Abraham shows no self-awareness. Judeo-Christian Abraham grows in self-awareness as he walks with God. Thus Islam does not focus on the struggle in the journey of faith but on mindless obedience.

Islam puts emphasis on Abraham's acquiescence, but Judaism portrays him as having a struggle to follow the path of faith. The Koran points to Abraham as a perfect prophet while the Bible reveals both his humanity and mistakes in the journey. Whenever he went astray, God intervened with a promise, a covenant, and a sign. When God commends Abraham after saving Lot, Abraham responds by declaring he can't truly be blessed if he doesn't have any children. Then God dramatically gave a picture of Abraham's future generations including captivity in a foreign land and a dramatic return from there.

This expansion in horizon can be viewed as a reward for admitting his struggle to believe the earlier promise God had made about being the father of many nations. The tottering faith of Abraham is slowly being transformed into towering faith. Abraham made a series of mistakes, and though God is not pleased with these choices by Abraham, He is willing to allow the consequences to develop. But He continues working with Abraham.

This towering giant in faith shows another evidence of his struggle to follow God's rules. He submits to his wife, Sarah, and condones her wronging toward Hagar and Ishmael. Even there Abraham is so human and frail, a far cry from the perfect Abraham of the Koran. Hagar is afflicted by Sarah, just like the Israelites in Egypt are afflicted by the Pharaoh. Both flee to the desert . . . to be precise to the wilderness of Shur where the Israelites arrived after crossing the Red sea. Like Moses, the leader of the Israelites, Hagar learns directly from God about the great future of her child. The sign of the covenant, circumcision, is given to Abraham first and to Ishmael second. Isaac is not even in the picture. But the covenant is expansive. It is not limited to Abraham's physical descendants. It is available to anyone who is part of Abraham's household. God maintains a balance between Isaac and Ishmael. Isaac receives the land through his mother's schemes; Ishmael receives God's blessing through his mother's surrender.

Abraham's life story in retelling is open to reinterpretation. For Islam the stories told about him after he died became more important in forming history than the stories told about him while he lived. In Christianity the reverse is true. The stories told about Abraham while he lived became more important in forming leaders of the Christian faith. Islamic, Christian, and Jewish traditions all play significant events in fulfilling God's prophetic calendar and agenda at the macro level.

The agent of the original sin, the archangel Lucifer, now known as Satan, was a formidable adversary to defeat. The story of Abraham, Isaac, and Jacob, is a history where God attains multiple objectives. The complete annihilation of the opposing forces was to be accomplished along with populating the planet with the knowledge of God. The legions of evil, mentioned in the Bible, are demons or fallen angels that serve Satan as powerful entities including Chemosh, Ba'al, Bel, Nego, Ashtar, the bull god, the fish god, and even the falling stars. God's plan is to destroy the Kingdom of Darkness led by Satan.

The Captain of the Hosts of heaven was the leader of the invading forces. Jesus became the Christ when he conquered death. To the astonishment of the armies of heaven Jesus came as the son of man, the seed of the woman as promised to Eve. When He was on the cross bleeding to death in His weakness, the armies of heaven could not understand how or why the wisdom of God was represented by the weakness of their Captain on the cross.

The story of Abraham, Isaac, and Jacob was set for revealing the story of God the Father, His only begotten Son, Jesus, and the pure Spirit of heaven, the Holy Spirit. If we accept the motif of war between the Kingdom of Light and the Kingdom of Darkness, then the Angel of the Lord, who accepted worship from Abraham and Moses and the Captain of the hosts who appeared to Joshua (5:13-15), becomes an expression of the pre-incarnate Christ. As the Captain of the Armies of heaven, He not only demanded worship, He came to give the order of the battle. Both to Jacob (Gen.32: 24-32) and to Manoah (Judges 13:17-18) the angel refused to reveal his name though he was careful in blessing them to advance the purpose of God. Centuries later, Isaiah wrote about the wonderful name of this coming seed of Abraham as 'Wonderful Counselor, Mighty God, Eternal Father, Prince of Peace'(Is.9:6).

The types and shadow of reality hidden in the Old Testament assume great significance when we look at the conflict Islam has with the Judeo-Christian narrative. God dealt with humanity in Adam, Noah, Abraham, Moses, David, and Jesus, but these six covenants not only get shuffled and reinterpreted within Islam, but Islam also adds a new covenant . . . the covenant with Muhammad.

There is no indication yet of how God will deal with the Prophet of Islam. Within the Christian world view it can allegorically be considered as part of the mystery of evil. To understand this we need to explore the symbolism of the Bible hidden in the expression 'God of Abraham, Isaac and Jacob.'

# Symbols
# in the Bible

---

# Chapter Twelve

In Islam's on-going conflict with the West, the Western media has not shown the courage to articulate the event on 9/11 as the conflict between the Islamic consciousness and Western nation-states. As most of the media reports indicated, the choice of September 11 has been portrayed as a play on 911, which is the telephone number for emergency services in the United States. By denying the religious symbolism in Islam's conflict with the West, the media has presented Islam as a religion of moderation that was hijacked by the terrorists. This portrayal of Islam, helped by the fundamental denial of spirituality in the Western media, is best seen in their reluctance to report surah 9:111 as a primary reason for the selection of the date for launching the attack on the World Trade Center. Islam as a tool has almost destroyed the concept of nation-states!

That surah clearly states that "Allah hath purchased of the Believers their persons and their goods; for theirs (in return) is the garden (of paradise): They fight in his cause And slay and are slain:…" Though it would be wrong to portray Islam as a religion of war, the Islamists, unlike the ordinary Muslims take the injunction to fight the *Kafir* (unbeliever) as seriously as the texts commands. Ordinary Muslims take it as a symbolism of Islam that needs to be interpreted by the scholars before put into practice. But the West needs to understand the power of symbols embedded in the consciousness of religious believers even as they discover the carefully distributed symbolism in the

Bible.

In the book of Genesis the Bible explains carefully that God wanted to be known as the God of Abraham, Isaac, and Jacob. Embedded in this title is the concept of a triune God who works in history to restore humanity to Himself. The story of Abraham is recorded in chapters 11-25 in Genesis. Abraham is called to walk with God in chapter 12 and then he makes a series of mistakes as he pursues the lonely walk of faith. His mistakes include going to Egypt, sleeping with Hagar, suggesting to God to choose Ishmael, calling his wife his sister to protect himself, and not understanding the covenant of circumcision as opposed to the love-relation of faith.

Yet God saw that Abraham would pass the test of faith involving his promised son, Isaac (Genesis 22:2), even though Ishmael was alive. Regardless of the claims of the Koran, we learn from the Biblical account that Abraham had no relationship with Ishmael after he was sent out with his mother Hagar. By taking his child of promise, Isaac, he was obeying God in the deepest sense. But God through Abraham was embedding a symbol of faith in human consciousness stating clearly that He was not like other gods who desired human sacrifices.

The God of Abraham was starting the redemptive history promised through the seed of the woman. The story of Hagar, Lot, and Sarah remain as rational subplots within the main story. Until the story of Christ is completed, God's demand that Abraham sacrifice Isaac remained an illogical test of faith as Isaac was the child of promise.

The Abrahamic covenant of circumcision was extended to Ishmael, but God did not fully reveal His true purposes for Isaac and the redemptive history till the books of Hebrews and Romans were written. The fact that all three patriarchs, Abraham, Isaac, and Jacob, lived as nomads in tents is a central observation of the Hebrew's author (Heb. 11). They shared an expectation of a city not built by human hands. The three Patriarchs also taught their generations about their experience of Elohim, the God of Israel, who gave names to followers as He became a new experience to each one. By contrast Islam teaches that Ishmael became a resident in the city of Mecca which is a type for the city of man.

Isaac, the least flamboyant of the three patriarchs, appears as an almost colorless character till we observe that he alone among the three had the 'one man-one woman' model relationship. His whole life is summarized in almost three and a half chapters by the author of Genesis. He was a type for the suffering servant who did what was right before the Father in picture perfect obedience. The longest chapter in Genesis is dedicated to his marriage to

Rebekah.

This divinely ordained marriage seemed to be a failure as the twins born to them became competitors. The apparently nobler of the two, the outdoor hunter Esau, gets a raw deal as the brooding brother Jacob beats him in the game of inheritance. Only when we look at the picture of Esau through divine perspective are we able to see the gravity of unbelief. Through unbelief Esau chose to sell what he had received as a gift from God. By disregarding his birthright he chose his will over God's plan. Jacob sought God out of necessity, but he was saved by seeking God. At the human level this story makes no sense except when we read the history of the church through the lens of Jacob's life. The power of the embedded symbol is fully revealed by Jacob in chapter 49 when he becomes the first great human prophet, the Hebrew seer who peers into time accurately to report the future.

Jacob was forced to trust God because he really was not trained at home in the ways of God. As a cheat, when he runs from his own home and culture, he truly becomes the ever-present refugee in the human story. He was a prototype of the wandering Jew, the Huguenots, the Pilgrim fathers, the Puritans, and many others who were forced to trust the unseen God because of the wandering nature of their journey on earth. But Jacob was not ready to become a spiritual man like Abraham, his grandfather, or Isaac, his father, because he was a quintessential crook till he was transformed.

Unlike his unbelieving brother, Esau, Jacob did not have a propensity to immorality or even self-direction. He turned to God because life made him a wanderer almost like Cain but without bloodguilt. As he slept at Bethel on his journey to the grandmaster of deception, his uncle Laban, he was visited by the presence of God. Almost fifteen chapters in Genesis are dedicated to the story of Jacob. The entire story is dedicated to a hidden order revolving around his subconscious, his character flaws, his largely complicated marital life, and the families of his children.

In Jacob's story God appears to choose him over Esau just as God chose Isaac over Ishmael. God introduced Himself in a dream as the God of Abraham, the God of Isaac, and promises that the land where he was sleeping belonged to his descendants (Genesis 28:13). But God does not introduce himself as the God of Ishmael, posing a great dilemma for the Muslims.

It was not the promise of the land to Jacob that was pregnant with symbolism. He received the promise of a seed through which all the families of the earth would be blessed as God had told Abraham earlier (chapter 12). The greater promise was the presence of God that will accompany Jacob till God completes the promises made to him (Gen.28:15). What was implicit in

God's promise to Abraham becomes explicit in God's promise to Jacob. Independent of what Jacob does in response, God becomes the promise giver and the promise keeper. Even this promise makes total sense only after the descending of the Holy Spirit on the church and the book of Romans.

Jacob, who had cheated his father and elder brother, gets cheated many times by his father-in-law. God patiently waits for Jacob to become a man who sought God like Abraham had done. It was the intervention of his God that saved him from the wrath of Laban as he tried to escape from the clutches of a monopolist who kept changing the wages of his son-in-law. True capitalism was yet to be invented because tribalism did not honor the rights of the individual.

The symbolism of the two wives of Jacob, their competition, and the addition of concubines to win the competition, makes complete sense only after Paul completed the book of Galatians. Jacob had realized the goodness of a God who was able to keep him from being destroyed while he profoundly became aware of his own sinfulness (Gen. 32:10). But the biggest surprise of the story was not the escape of the entire family of Jacob at the brook of Jabok but the appearance of a mysterious angel who wrestled with Jacob almost till day break (Gen. 32:24-32). This angel had appeared to his grandfather, Abraham, to promise the birth of his father Isaac. The angel refuses to give His own name to Jacob, (Gen. 32:29) but he changes Jacob's name to Israel. The key to what happened to Jacob in his wrestling match was given to another prophet Hosea (12:4) as tears of self-awareness and repentance.

The new order God wanted to inaugurate starts with repentance following a profound self-awareness of sin. In the entire Old Testament whenever the Prophets spoke of God's justice it revealed man's need for holiness, not just repentance but the true change of the heart of man as in Jacob. The transformation of Jacob was forcefully started through the sinfulness of his own children starting with Simeon and Levi who deceived and murdered an entire village (chapter 34). Forced to go back to Bethel out of fear, like when he was escaping the wrath of his brother, Esau, Jacob again received the promise of a name change and the land from God (35:10-12). If he had any doubts about his own name change, it was completely removed as God once again introduced himself as the God of Abraham and Isaac (35:12).

The biggest reversals of Jacob's life were yet to come. His favorite wife, Rachel, died soon after fulfilling his own judgment (Gen.31:32) revealing that Rachel had not understood the faith of her husband or his ancestors. The death of Rachel made his children Joseph and Benjamin more important than the other ten, setting the family up for greater disaster. The rest of the brothers hated Joseph for many reasons including the dreams and the discrimination of their father, Jacob. The author of Genesis seemed to paint the story of Jacob intricately into the story of Joseph as Jacob gets addressed as Israel (Gen. 37:3,13; 46:1,8) while he is called Jacob elsewhere. In the story of Joseph the author seems to hide Jacob till he becomes the overcoming prince of God as in Israel.

Unlike in his own past when he escaped from the Promised Land, Jacob carefully seeks the will of God before he embarks on his journey to Egypt (Gen. 46:1-5). God takes special care to address him as Jacob before He promises him His presence and Jacob's eventual return to the Promised Land. It would be granted only after his death as Joseph had his body returned by his descendants (Gen. 46:4). Unlike both Abraham and Isaac who went or tried to go to Egypt outside of God's perfect will, Jacob was asked to go to Egypt by his God. Not only did Jacob go to Egypt but unlike his grandfather, Abraham, he blessed Pharaoh, the most powerful man on earth (Gen. 47:10). The transformation of the wanderer Jacob was almost completed by being the spiritual man he had to be, by blessing the Pharaoh. But the last step, becoming a seer who saw the future of his generations, was still to come.

The question of true spirituality is closely related to the name and experience of God. God appears guarded in the narrative about giving His name to an unprepared Jacob when they struggled with each other at the brook of Jabok. But over his lifetime that changed as God became very personal. Though there are many kinds of theogonic myths which show how gods came into being or men became gods, there are none in world history where God becomes man to show the path of powerlessness.

If the name of the angel was kept a secret in the story of Jacob, it was partly because he had not exhibited the *justness of the faith* his grandfather had. The angel wanted to bless Jacob at the brook, but Jacob was not ready yet. Unlike his aged grandfather, Abraham, with his childless wife Sarah, who believed the promise of God that he would be the father of many nations, Jacob was not ready to fully trust God. Therefore God was not yet willing to trust him with His name.

In Egypt towards the end of his life as he adopts Joseph's children, Ephraim and Manasseh, he calls the God of his fathers his shepherd, and he distinctly mentions the angel who redeemed him from all evil (Gen.48:15-16). Not only does he mention the angel, but he also asks this angel to bless these two lads. The Christology of the New Testament had already started for Jacob, though he did not know the name or the identity of the angel. When he blessed Judah, his fourth son, he saw a future descendant of Judah who would be named Shiloh and all the peoples of the world would obey Him (Gen. 49:10). As Israel the patriarch, he saw the scepter, the symbol of a king, not ever departing from this future king. But he also saw this king tying his donkey to a vine (Gen. 49:1a). Not only did Jesus ride on a donkey, but he also pictured himself as the true vine (John 15). What is more fascinating about what Jacob saw is the second part (Gen. 49:11b) where the robe of this future king is dipped in the blood of grapes. The dual symbolism cannot be missed again.

The blood of grapes equally points to the Eucharist table, the Passover blood represented by wine as well as the theme of Isaiah 63. As the king of Israel, when Christ comes from Edom (modern Jordan) to establish justice on the planet Earth, the prophet Isaiah asks the rhetorical question, *"Why is Your apparel red, And Your garments like one who treads in the winepress?"* (Isa. 63:2). This question is answered as this future king of Israel judges the nations:

> *"I have trodden the winepress alone, And from the peoples no one was with Me. For I have trodden them in My anger, And trampled them in My fury; Their blood is sprinkled upon My garments, And I have stained all My robes. For the day of vengeance is in My heart, And the year of My redeemed has come"* (Isa. 63:3-4).

Unlike other myths found in all major religions, the myth of Judeo-Christian origin when sought out earnestly by humanity becomes verity through the logic embedded in the Bible. Just like Islamic thought, this too produces an altered state of consciousness in the New Testament believer through the symbols embedded in the Torah. The Christian is challenged to discover life in Christ through the ancient scriptures. As the followers of Christ obey, their calculative mind, the basis for the world, becomes a contemplative mind as found in Jacob. This contemplative mind is the beginning of the spiritual mind which is the mind of Christ as Paul saw it. The cross teaches the contemplative mind as the way to the mind of Christ.

The life of Jacob is no more mythical as the human consciousness gets transformed by the growing knowledge of God though the cross of Christ. It becomes clearer by meditating on the triune nature of God found in the expression God of Abraham, Isaac, and Jacob. Jacob's life was progressively miserable from the time of the appearance of the Angel of the Lord till he found the greatness of his beloved son, Joseph in Egypt. This is allegorical to the acceptance of Christ into the heart of a New Testament believer, only to progressively discover the power of Christ in the hidden divine order of things.

But Jacob was not the only person visited by this Angel of the Lord, the pre-incarnate Christ, as seen from the story of Hagar. As an Egyptian maid to Sarah (Gen.16), Hagar had no ability to withstand the plan of her master sleeping with her because it was with the connivance of her mistress. But when she conceived, she found pride in herself which made her despise her mistress. But Sarah, with the consent of Abraham, mistreated Hagar, literally forcing her to flee from them. The mysterious Angel of the Lord appeared to her and commanded her to return back to vindictive Sarah. As it was his practice, this Angel named the child Ishma-el, after one of the names of God, El-ohim. But like her master and the father of her child, Abraham, would do later, Hagar gave a name to this becoming Angel: El-roi (a God who sees). By faith Hagar achieved intimacy with Elohim which Abraham was to learn in the Isaac saga. But Isaac had not been born yet!

Hagar was more privileged than Abraham and Sarah because she met the pre-incarnate Christ before Sarah did. At least fourteen years later, after Isaac was born, Hagar and her son Ishmael were driven out by Sarah because Ishmael mocked Isaac, the true heir to Abraham according to God's promise. The two individuals, Ishmael and Isaac, central characters to Pauline analysis of grace and the life of the Spirit in Galatians represent two types of consciousness. Ishmael, representing the law and slavery to rituals and codes, opposes the life of the Spirit and promises of God represented by Isaac. It is ironic to note that in Galatians (4:21-26) Hagar, Ishmael, and Isaac are mentioned by name but not Sarah. The place of the free woman, Sarah, is taken by the heavenly Jerusalem who is the bride of Christ and possibly the City of God. The entire subplot of Hagar and Ishmael in the story of Abraham is used as an illustration by Paul to teach the mechanics of the life of the Spirit, which was the whole purpose of the life of Jacob, the patriarch who became Israel.

Neither the symbolism in these stories can be denied nor can they be called myths because of the ring of truth echoed through these events as found in the history of tribal societies, especially of the nomadic tribes of the Arabian Desert. As Abraham struggles with the decision of having to send Hagar and Ishmael away, God steps into his life with a promise that places Isaac in a unique position as the descendant of Abraham (Gen. 21:12). It is through Isaac God promises to name the descendants of Abraham, not through the children of Ishmael. But God is happy to honor Ishmael because he is Abraham's descendant (21:13) but not for redemptive history. Again in the midst of another severe trial in the life of Hagar, the same Angel of the Lord

# Islam's Conflict with the West

calls out from heaven to direct the steps of their life as mother and son. In a very real sense Hagar is considered a blessed woman like Mary, the mother of Jesus. Unlike Mary, her son had no great role to play in redemptive history.

In other words, the Bible in the book of Genesis denies the possibility of a covenant emerging through the lineage of Ishmael. The covenants God makes with humanity from Abraham, to Moses, to David, and to Jesus stay within the lineage of Isaac. The covenant with Abraham and the covenants made with Adam and Noah gave Ishmaelite tribes the right to three of the ancient covenants of the Bible. The last covenant offered through the life of Jesus is the universal covenant which has only two symbolic rituals. Though profound, both have simple elegance to them in baptism and the Lord's Table.

The symbolism of Islam differs radically. The symbolism in the Prophet Muhammad's naming the God of Abraham, Isaac, and Jacob, as also the God of Isma-il needs to be understood carefully. In Arabic, the name Isma-il is derived from samia, the word to hear.

The Koran mentions a covenant of Abraham and Isma-il with Allah (surah 2:125). ". . . we covenanted with Abraham and Ismail that they should sanctify my house for those who compass it round, or use it as a retreat, or bow, or prostrate themselves." The city mentioned here is Mecca and the house is the Kaaba. Through tragic symbolism, Islam, a religion committed to removing the worship of false gods (idols), ends up urging their followers to go around a physical structure made of stone containing an ancient black stone mounted in silver. It not only adds a false covenant, but it gets their believers to follow a lie that is essentially negated in their own doctrine. How could this happen? The Koran was contradicting itself.

Who was this angel that directed the Prophet of Islam?

There are at least three possibilities on the identity based on the Islamic symbolism and the Bible. The primary gods of that region of the world were Bel, Ba'al, and the moon god. Though the Islamic tradition ascribes to the Prophet many miracles outside of the Koran, the only major miracle alluded to in the Koran is the splitting of the moon. In surah 54:1-3 the idea of confronting his polytheistic critics with his divine mission is accomplished by showing two different parts of the moon in the heavens. In the Islamic tradition this miracle was produced to remove any lingering doubts in the mind of the followers of the moon god. Later his inner circle refers to this collective experience outside of the Koran in their traditions.

This supposed miracle is a clue to the identity of the angel who appeared to the Prophet because the symbol of the crescent appears on most of Islam's holy sites. These objects of Islam, the most radical monotheistic system

108

devised by man, not only became central to worship, but they also hide the identity of the angel who appeared to the Prophet.

The certainty with which the Prophet viewed the failed mission of the Jewish nation has been negated by the return of the Jew to Israel in the 20th century. The return of the Jew not only negates Islam's view of a failed Jewish nation, but it is becoming the direct fulfillment of the Old Testament prophecy. The primary response exhibited by the Arab nations is not to question the revelation in the Koran, but to concentrate their forces and efforts in an attempt to destroy the nation of Israel. It is in this mindset that biblical prophecy and the city of Jerusalem assumes great importance for the students of prophecy.

Though Jerusalem is not mentioned in the Koran even once, most Muslims consider Jerusalem as their third holy city even after the fact that the Prophet changed the direction of the prayer from Jerusalem to Mecca. The primary reason for Jerusalem comes from a word play (with interpretation) where the Koran mentions in surah 17:1 the Masjid Al Aqsa, the farthest mosque. When this surah was given by the Prophet (before 632), there were neither Muslims in Jerusalem nor a Mosque. Yet when the Arab armies came to conquer Jerusalem in 638 they assumed they would find the farthest mosque there. When they found no mosque in Jerusalem, they built a mosque to prove the prophetic element in the surah. Actually after that event, except for the battles between the Crusaders and Saladin, Jerusalem never achieved any importance in Arab history. Even with the Turks it did not gain any importance but for a brief period when Napoleon tried to conquer it in his invasion from Egypt.

When the British ruled Palestine from 1917-1918, they elevated Jerusalem to be Palestines's most important city and placed their administration there. Previously for the Islamic Turks it was just a neglected outpost. But in the 20th century, it became the symbol for the conflict between the returning Jew and their ancient Arab brothers. The focus of this struggle, centered on 35 acres of land on the Temple Mount, has taken a different meaning with the symbols of the Cross and the Crescent Moon. It was in the region of this mount Abraham offered Isaac (Mount Moriah) and much later God the Father offered his Son, Jesus Christ. To give credence to the ancient conflict described in the Old Testament, the region seems to be getting ready for the finale of the conflict of the ages. No wonder, Prophet Jeremiah wrote:

> *"Behold, the days are coming," says the LORD, "that I will*
> *punish all who are circumcised with the uncircumcised— Egypt,*
> *Judah, Edom, the people of Ammon, Moab, and all who are in the*
> *farthest corners, who dwell in the wilderness. For all these nations*

*are uncircumcised, and all the house of Israel are uncircumcised*
*in the heart"* (Jer. 9:25-26).

Though God promised the land of Palestine to the Jew, it is certain when it comes to a renewed heart both the Jew and the Arab stand before God with an uncircumcised heart along with the Christian who is following his carnal nature.

What should be the Christian believers response to this challenge built on the conflict of these symbols?

# A Christian Response to Islam's Challenge

## Chapter Thirteen

The central conflict in the Bible regarding the name of God is hardly understood in the West now. John Kearney wrote in The New York Times (Jan.28, 2004), "My God is Your God" trying to convince the media and the Christians that Allah is the same God that Abraham worshipped. So he argued 'Allah' should be translated as God in English because he saw Allah as the 'shared God of Judaism, Christianity, and Islam.' In Arabic the word Allah stands for God, but Allah in Islam represents a different character than the God of the Bible who is the God of Abraham, Isaac, and Jacob. In Islam, not only is Allah known as the God of Ismail (Ishmael), but he is also the god who rejected the Jewish nation from fulfilling the divine purposes in their selection from the time of Abraham's call.

This difference is central to the current conflict between Islam and Christianity. It was anticipated by Jesus in the high priestly prayer found in John 17. As Jesus prays for the church in the final days of his earthly ministry, He clearly expounds the importance of the name of God. Jesus said,

> "I have manifested Your name to the men whom You have given Me out of the world. They were Yours, You gave them to Me, and they have kept Your word. Now they have known that all things which You have given Me are from You. For I have given to them the words which You have given Me; and they have received them, and have known surely that I came forth from You; and they have believed that You sent Me.

*"I pray for them. I do not pray for the world but for those whom You have given Me, for they are Yours. And all Mine are Yours, and Yours are Mine, and I am glorified in them. Now I am no longer in the world, but these are in the world, and I come to You. Holy Father, keep through Your name those whom You have given Me, that they may be one as We are. While I was with them in the world, I kept them in Your name. Those whom You gave Me I have kept; and none of them is lost except the son of perdition, that the Scripture might be fulfilled"* (Jn. 17:6-12).

Jesus not only thanked the Father for giving Him an opportunity to manifest His Name, but He also prayed that they would be kept in His Name by the power of the Father. Hidden in this prayer is the mystery in the concept of evil and the spiritual conflict that is focused on the Name of God.

In most Eastern cultures the name reveals the character of the person and his lineage. Also in the West the name often represents the family, at least the trade of the family. In spiritual context the name is not only representative of authority, but it also reveals character and identity.

When Moses, the author of Genesis, is addressed by God at the burning bush, God identifies Himself as "I Am," Yahweh (Ex. 3:14). This was written as the unpronounceable YHWH in Hebrew, translated as Jehovah in German, and is often written as LORD in English. As Abraham began his spiritual journey, one of the basic spiritual lessons he learned was to call on the name of the LORD (Gen.12:8, 13:4). But as Jewish prophets recognized, the nature of God is closely connected with His name. The prophet Zephaniah also saw the coming conflict regarding the name of God.

*"Therefore wait for Me," says the LORD, "Until the day I rise up for plunder; My determination is to gather the nations To My assembly of kingdoms, To pour on them My indignation, All My fierce anger; All the earth shall be devoured With the fire of My jealousy. For then I will restore to the peoples a pure language, That they all may call on the name of the LORD, To serve Him with one accord . . ."* (Zeph. 3:8-9).

A careful study of the Bible reveals sanctification, a major theme in the New Testament, as a necessary condition for people to call on the name of the Lord as Zephaniah prophesied.

Zephaniah declares the need for purity to call on the name of the Lord, just as he reveals the need to wait for the Lord to rise up as a witness against the nations and their gods. The theme of hidden evil which God is going to expose and destroy is central to all the prophets in the Old Testament. Just as the book of Genesis has a hidden order conforming to the expression of the

God of Abraham, Isaac, and Jacob, the entire Bible deals extensively with the concept of spiritual evil. Though this concept might be foreign to people in the 21st century, a central issue regarding evil is the differing experiences of humanity in experiencing the Names of God. Not only did God forbid worshipping other gods, but He expressed a necessary characteristic for true worship through His name, *for you shall worship no other god, for the LORD, whose name is Jealous, is a jealous God* (Ex. 34:14). The exclusive nature of His name provokes a zeal which shows God in the Bible guarding His name with power.

Jesus not only kept his disciples by the power of His name, but He revealed the true nature of God through the cross of Christ. God explicitly instructed Moses to teach the Israelites not to use the names of other gods by stating, *"make no mention of the name of other gods, nor let it be heard from your mouth"* (Ex. 23:13). As the problem of evil is solved, the Prophet Zechariah clearly states the conflict regarding the name of God will be finally put to rest. *And the LORD shall be King over all the earth. In that day it shall be—"The LORD is one," And His name one* (Zech. 14:9). Though it is not easy to understand this ancient conflict, which the Bible calls a mystery, it is fairly well laid out in many steps and stages that will unfold as this spiritual conflict gets resolved.

The Mystery of Lawlessness that Paul referred to in 2 Thessalonians 2:7 is going to be solved when the unseen host of wickedness that prompts the nations to act against the true God is finally defeated and destroyed or imprisoned. The mystery of God will be completed by the final actions that God will initiate against the unseen forces of wickedness in the heavenly places (Rev. 10:7). A large group of humanity who learned to walk with God as Father will be with Jesus as the final element of His wrath is poured out on these 'other gods' and their followers.

The absence of the concept of 'God as the Father' in Islam can be traced to the life of Ishmael who grew up with anger towards his father, but we can also trace it to the anger of the adversary (Satan) hidden in Islam towards the fatherhood of God. Though the concept of God as Father is dispersed through out the Old Testament as in Malachi (2:10), in Isaiah (63:16), in Jeremiah (31:9) and in other places, it was in the parable of the prodigal son (Luke 15) that the dramatic presentation of the Father was completed by Jesus. As the prodigal returns to the Father, Jesus drew a word picture that makes it difficult to view the Father as uninvolved. *But when he was still a great way off, his father saw him and had compassion, and ran and fell on his neck and kissed him* (Luke 15:20).

God choose to reveal His relational desire through sending His Son, but He also established Himself as the Father for all who would accept the Son so that He can call them sons and daughters of God. For a Muslim, one of the hardest hurdles to cross is to be daring enough to call God the Father. Since Islam is hostile to this concept, Christians ought to love them until they discover that God is truly love and relational as a father is in a family.

The root of the anger found in Islam partly stems from a distorted picture of the father. Since the father is not asked in Islam to develop a one man-one woman relationship, often he is missing in the formation of the character of a child. The concept of a father carefully training the child in the ways of God is missing in pure Islam. It is more of a religious adherence taught by a community, a collective form of orthopraxy. One of the most affirmed truths in the Bible is the concept of a faithful father who teaches the next generation to walk in the ways of God. God demanded this of Abraham.

The divine glory *(Kabod)* is to be taught by the fathers to their children. The display of Kabod with Moses and the Israelites at Sinai was such a beginning. This display of power before an entire community had great consequences in history starting with the Ten Commandments and the Pentateuch. The Prophet Isaiah recalled these events when he described the God *Who led them by the right hand of Moses, With His glorious arm, Dividing the water before them To make for Himself an everlasting name* (Isa. 63:12). Later John, the disciple, makes it clear that the glorious arm of God was Jesus Himself (Jn. 12:38). Though God was committed to creating an everlasting Name for Himself with Moses, as well as at the cross, He was revealing the full meaning in His glorious Name. This revelation of power at the Red Sea and powerlessness at the cross was independent of the obedience of the Jewish nation.

The display of power in a systemic sense, through the Names of God, is related to the story of Israel just as the display of powerlessness and humility of God is reserved for the church of Jesus Christ. It is in God's commitment to powerlessness in the experience of the cross that children of God can know Him as their father.

Islam denies the powerlessness of God at the cross by denying the cross and by trying to destroy the church of God in the countries where Muslims have imposed their ideology. They do not understand the coming judgment. They consider themselves successful because through persecution and oppression they have been able to prevent the growth of the church in their nations. But as the prophets throughout the Old Testament have indicated, God is forcefully going to display His power to the Islamic nations through the history of the tiny nation Israel in modern times.

Before the Bible was translated into the European history of the 16th century, the Catholic Church opposed it for centuries causing the great conflict which ended in the Reformation. Now it is the turn of Islam in the Middle East to unleash a great conflict where the ancient Garden of Eden and later the hanging gardens of Babylon existed. The nation of Israel, set up to destroy the spiritual forces of wickedness ruling that ancient geographical area, is going to be a conundrum for the historian in the immediate future.

After Moses and the great King David, when Jewish disobedience became a generational failure during the time of their latter kings, God warned them of national disaster. Ezekiel recorded God's sorrow:

> *Also I scattered them among the nations and they were dispersed throughout the lands. According to their ways and their deeds I judged them. When they came to the nations where they went, they profaned My holy name, because it was said of them, 'These are the people of the Lord; yet they have come out of His land. But I have concern for My holy name, which the house of Israel had profaned among the nations where they went* (Eze. 36:19-21).

But even in the Jewish disobedience God did not abandon His plan of redemption as He stated, *O house of Israel, that I am about to act, but for My holy name."* The promise continues in a dramatic fashion, *I will give you a new heart and put a new spirit within you; I will take the heart of stone out of your flesh and give you a heart of flesh. I will put My Spirit within you and cause you to walk in My statutes, and you will keep My judgments and do them. Then you shall dwell in the land that I gave to your fathers; you shall be My people, and I will be your God* (Ezek. 36:26-28).

The promise of being restored to their own land and having a renewed experience of God was given to the Jews long before the Second Temple was built and then destroyed. The Prophet Ezekiel in chapter 37 also described the dramatic account of how impossible it will look as the Jews return to the Promised Land. Dry bones that are gathered together with sinews, flesh, and skin, and finally life enters there as the breath of God falls on them. They are called 'an exceedingly great army.'

These events that Ezekiel saw have taken place from 1948 to 2005 in modern Israel as this tiny nation has become a military powerhouse that defeated the combined armies of 5 Arab nations many times. The purpose of this latter day revival was also given by Ezekiel. *"Then the nations which are left all around you shall know that I, the LORD, have rebuilt the ruined places and planted what was desolate. I, the LORD, have spoken it, and I will do it"* (Ezek. 36:36). But today the power of Islam prevents the knowledge of the living God from spreading among the nations. But the God of Abraham, Isaac, and Jacob has promised to remove that resistive force of Islam through catastrophic events.

Just as Islam is a religion of orthopraxy with legalism that opposes most of modernity, strife is going to increase in the nations that have Islam as a majority faith. The Bible insists that God is after human hearts that focus on a transforming relationship with Him which makes the practice of Christianity an act of continued love. Man can only relate to God in His powerlessness which makes the cross absolutely necessary for relating to a very powerful God who calls Himself holy and a consuming fire. Any impurity in humanity will destroy us as we relate to this holy God of Abraham, Isaac, and Jacob unless He comes to us in powerlessness.

The church teaches relational truth in experience by understanding the truth about God and life through the written scriptures. On the contrary Islam insists on scriptures without making truth relational and is enforced by the sword and fear. In a definite sense Islam is the antithesis of everything that Christ taught except for social orthodoxy.

The lack of the concept of perfectible perfection in Islam forces it to enforce uniformity through the sword, creating an atmosphere of fear and violence. Unless these errors are confronted and rejected, Islam stands very little chance of being moderated. To lovingly confront Islam with the cross of Christ will not be possible without the power of the Holy Spirit. Just as the Koran denies the cross, the Bible points to the cross as the central reality in the redemptive scheme chalked out by God in Jesus Christ.

To grasp and to learn the way of the cross, God sent the Holy Spirit. The Holy Spirit through the church deals with human transformation as God's judgment is completed in history. Thus we see God allowing great freedom to Islam to fulfill the dark prophetic sayings of judgment from the Old Testament on to a Christ-rejecting-world. Filled with a missionary zeal with a whole-hearted commitment to senseless violence, Islamists pose a far greater threat to the Western civil societies than communism ever was. Having lost a significant portion of their spiritual heritage that provided the political freedoms to the West, the beautiful side of evil has created a deception through Islam that cannot be exposed in the West without a deeper understanding of the Bible.

As Christians, our response is to love our Muslim brothers and sisters who are the sons and daughters of Ishmael, Esau, and Lot's daughters even as we prayerfully expose the myth of equating the god of Islam with the God of Abraham, Isaac, and Jacob. This confrontation hidden in revealing the true name of God and experiencing God through Christ is the purpose of human history.

# Islam's Conflict with the West

# Glossary

---

**Ahmedi (or Ahmediyas):** Followers of Mirza Ghulam Ahmed from the 19th century;
Alawi or Alawites - Mostly in Syria
Khoja; Bhora; Isma'ilis - Mostly in India and South Asia.

**Caliph:** The religious and secular head of all Islam.

**Fatrah:** The extended break between Muhammad's first and second visit from his angel of revelation.

**Hadith:** Traditional sayings and acts of Mohammad

**Hajj:** One of the five pillares of Islam. The pilrimage to Mecca

**Hanif:** Pre-Islamic Arabs who believed in the existance of one unseen god.

**Iblis:** The Arabic word for Satan. During the Hajj, in the small town of Mina, pilgrims symbolically cast pebbles at pillars that represent Iblis and evil.

**I'jaz:** The "impossibility" of translating the Koran because of the allusive and concise style of Arabic used in its authorship.

**Imam:** Muslim leader in the mosque and community. Often the preacher.

**Iqra:** The word commanding Muhammad to read, proclaim or recite as dictated by his angel of revelation.

**Islam:** A religion that appeared in the form of a book, the Koran. In Arabic it is considered the word of God. Islam means "submission."

**Jinn:** Evil spiritual beings in the desert made up of smokeless fire.

**Kaaba (Ka'bah):** An ancient pre-Islamic shrine in the city of Mecca. This shrine was cleansed of idols by Muhammad and now is used for worship where *tawaf* (the circling of the Kaaba) is done. It is a symbol of the oneness and centrality of God as taught in the doctrine of one God, *Tawhid* (also called *al Kalaam*).

**Kafir:** An unbeliever in Islam

**Rashidun:** "The Rightly Guided Ones" referring to the first four caliphs.

**Rasul:** An Apostle of God

**Sharia (Shari'ah):** The sacred law of Islam as found in the Koran, sunnah, and hadith.

**Shiite:** The second largest Islamic sect also known as (Shi'atu Ali), "the party for Ali," which had a different vision for the Ummah. They view the caliphate as an imamate or "leadership" which should stay in the family of the Prophet.

**Sufi:** Islamic mysticism which includes many divergent Shiite groups. A list of Sunni movements with Sufi influences include: Hanbalis, Shafis, Malikis, and Hanafis.

**Sunnah:** The practices of the Prophet.

**Sunni:** The largest sect in Islam known as (ahl al-sunnah wa-l-jama'ah), "the people of custom and community" who believe in the elective principle to decide the leaders of Islam (caliph) after Mohammed.

# Glossary

**Surahs:** The 114 chapters of the Koran which are divided into two broad categories: those revealed in Mecca (earlier and shorter) and those revealed in Medina (longer and full of details with specific legal, social, and political situations and often endorse violence). They are divided into ayahs or verses. Thus (2:20) means surah 2 and ayah 20. Surah 2 with 282 verses is the longest and surahs 103, 108, and 110 have three verses each making them the shortest.

**Tariquas:** Brotherhoods; ways or different techniques.

**Tawaf:** The circling of the Kaaba seven time during the hajj and kissing of the black stone set in its wall.

**Tawhid (al Kalaam):** The doctrine of one God

**Ummah** is the community of believers whose identity is dictated by the sacred law.

**Yazidis:** Ethnic Kurds who worship fallen angels. They call Satan the Peacock Angel, *Ta'us*.

# Islam's Conflict with the West

# Appendix

---

**CHARTING A FAITH BY NUMBERS:**

Some 40 percent of Muslims live in South and Southeast Asia where Islam was carried by soldiers and traders. Thirty percent live in Africa whose north became part of the Muslim world within a century of the death of Muhammad.

**NUMBERS IN MILLIONS:**

| | | |
|---|---|---|
| Indonesia | = | 181. |
| Pakistan | = | 141 |
| India | = | 124 |
| Bangladesh | = | 111 |
| Turkey | = | 66 |
| Egypt | = | 66 |
| Iran | = | 65 |
| Nigeria | = | 63 |
| China | = | 38 |
| Algeria | = | 31 |
| Ethiopia | = | 29 |
| Morocco | = | 29 |

| | | |
|---|---|---|
| Afghanistan | = | 27 |
| Iraq | = | 23 |
| Sudan | = | 22 |
| Uzbekistan | = | 22 |
| Saudi Arabia | = | 21 |
| Yemen | = | 18 |
| Syria | = | 15 |
| Tanzania | = | 13 |
| Russia | = | 12 |
| Malaysia | = | 12 |
| Mali | = | 10 |
| Tunisia | = | 10 |
| Senegal | = | 9 |
| Niger | = | 8 |
| Azerbaijan | = | 8 |
| Somalia | = | 7 |
| Kazakhstan | = | 7 |
| Guinea | = | 6 |
| Burkina Faso | = | 6 |
| United States | = | 6 |
| Tajikistan | = | 5 |
| Congo, Dem.Rep. | = | 5 |
| Libya | = | 5 |
| Turkeministan | = | 5 |
| Jordan | = | 5 |
| Cote D'Ivoire | = | 4 |
| Chad | = | 4 |
| Cameroon | = | 4 |